new 3rd edition

BMW

Classic 5 series 1972-2003

Marc Cranswick

Also from Veloce Publishing –

www.veloce.co.uk

First published 2002, new edition published August 2017, paperback edition published August 2021 by Veloce Publishing Limited, Veloce House, Parkway Farm Business Park, Middle Farm Way, Poundbury, Dorchester DT1 3AR, England.
Fax 01305 250479 / e-mail info@veloce.co.uk / web www.veloce.co.uk or www.velocebooks.com.
ISBN: 978-1-787117-75-4 UPC: 6-36847-01775-0

NEW 3RD EDITION

BMW

Classic 5 series 1972-2003

VELOCE

Marc Cranswick

CONTENTS

FOREWORDS

By Kevin Bird
and
Allen Hardy

BMW TUNING AROUND THE WORLD

I was delighted to be asked to write this foreword. It's fitting that the amazing early developments of BMW cars be committed to paper. Although my own work began in the days of the E28, my earliest memories of BMW cars are related to the forerunners of the E12, the 2800 and fabulous 3.0si saloons of the late 1960s. The Birds Garage business was one of the very first BMW dealers in the UK, so I was lucky to ride as a passenger in these often enthusiastically driven beasts.

It's absolutely clear that the evolution of the 5 Series has been the envy of the motoring manufacturers' world. Even the mighty Mercedes-Benz brand has had to accept that its mid-range cars are all too often second best when it comes to 'executive class' motors.

The over-riding characteristic that made BMWs most special was their sporting nature, and this is what originally attracted me, and continues to keep my eye focussed on the brand. To be able to take some of the finest German creations and hone them to a driver's exacting specification is a real pleasure, although it's not simply a case of bolting on some aftermarket products.

When we started tuning the 5 back in the early '80s, there was only one UK firm already in the marketplace, that being Tom Walkinshaw Racing, which had already formed a strong allegiance with Alpina. To us, the concept of taking standard BMW cars and tuning them for better performance was highly exciting, but rather than start from scratch, we engaged with the firm Hartge in Germany, which had a ready made tuning programme for the entire BMW range.

Whereas Alpina always seemed to have a gentleman's agreement with BMW, Hartge was absolutely independent, and never restricted by the factory in what it could deliver to the market. Although I didn't notice at the time, it appears that if Alpina came up with a conversion package, Hartge would always go one step further, producing a more powerful variant.

This strategy ultimately put Hartge out of reach to all but the most affluent enthusiasts, given the costs of tweakery on cars like the E28 M5, and the later amazingly expensive concept of inserting larger capacity engines under the bonnet.

For our part, we concentrated on delivering conservative and reliable, but tangible, improvements in engine and chassis performance. The bolt on aerodynamic 'improvements' never really proved attractive to our customers, so we left that to what has now become the largest sector of the so-called 'aftermarket tuning' industry.

I suspect our success is largely due to our genuine understanding of the BMW marque. BMW produce beautifully designed machines, and we concentrate on only a few areas that can be truly improved for enthusiastic drivers.

Kevin Bird of Birds Garage, UK Hartge Performance Partner

TUNING BMW'S 5 SERIES IN THE 'GOLDEN AGE' – CREATING AMERICA'S FIRST TUNER BMWS (1975-85)

Enthusiasts now take it for granted that BMW 5 Series is an exciting car to drive

This wasn't always so. When the then-new 530i reached California in 1975, the 3.0Si was still in showrooms, so comparisons were inevitable. The Bavaria and its fellow E3 variants, including the 3.0Si, had garnered accolades, with their light weight, elegant lines, and dazzling performance. By comparison, the US-version 530i was burdened with big bumpers, thermal reactors, and a soft suspension. To many, this seemed a step backward for the marque.

At H&B, customers prompted us to tweak the 530i as we had the similarly under-tuned 320i. It didn't seem practical to make the bigger cars lighter, but we could improve performance and handling; so we set about in that direction. In 1979, the arrival of the lambda sond and catalytic converters gave us the option of turbocharging. Suddenly, we had a serious driver's car in a mid-size sedan package.

We dropped off such a car for testing at *Road & Track*, where they expressed skepticism. When we picked it up, the attitude was one of appreciation. The same car turned quite a few heads in Detroit when tested by *Car and Driver*.

Only a couple of years later, BMW produced a 3.5-litre 'Motorsport' M535i on the E12 chassis; and by the mid '80s, there was the familiar, if still rare, M535i on the E28 chassis. From then to the present, BMW has sustained a line of performance-tuned 5 Series cars, occupying a market niche which simply didn't exist before. Many of these have become collectibles, and for good reason: they continue to be fabulous driver's cars, and rare.

Looking back to the late '70s and early '80s, this was a golden age for tuners. We had 'de-tuned' models in need of tweaking, and had a strong roster of suppliers to support our efforts: aerospace companies, metal foundries and fabricators, small suppliers of all sorts. The US dollar was strong, but not too strong, so the industrial base had not yet been decimated. By the mid '80s, however, all that began to change. The rising US dollar caused the demise of our small industrial suppliers, while stricter emission regulations – especially in California – created high legal and financial barriers for tuners. In hindsight, the late '70s and early '80s were a great time to be tweaking the BMW 5 Series. And H&B had a lot of fun doing it.

For their help in that process, we want to thank Precision Metal Casting, Hans Hermann of Drake Engineering; Bob Keane of Keane Fuel Systems; Sway-Away; Wolfgang of Midway Pattern; Precision Spring Company; all the people at Bilstein, especially Doug Robertson and Buzz in racing applications, and John Slagle and his colleagues at BBS Racing. Of all these, only the last two are still around to help tuners like us.

H&B founder Allen Hardy

INTRODUCTION

1981 BMW 528i outside BMW HQ München. (Courtesy Ulrich Thieme)

The 5 Series is like a good secretary: everyone wants one. So stated James May in his BBC *Top Gear* debut appearance, when covering a story on the E39 5 Series' replacement.

For many years, the BMW 3 Series has been seen as BMW's most popular car. However, for even longer it is the 5 Series that has proven to be Munchen's most profitable executive model, striking that perfect balance between sales and higher mark-up price.

The 5 Series was sound business based on enthusiast-directed sports saloons, and eventually, wagons. Larger, more refined developments of the type of cars that people expected from BMW. Expansion beyond the niche saw the production of diesel models, and practicality saw the 2002 range's Touring concept dusted off. Exclusivity was provided by performance tuners – very necessary, once BMWs began appearing everywhere.

This proliferation of tuners prompted the creation of BMW's own M cars. In the beginning, BMW Motorsport had looked after the company's racing activities, before eventually offering bespoke 5 Series to wealthy clientele and racing drivers. Next came the formally offered M cars, which were very effective publicity generators.

The E60 5 Series ended BMW's 'business as usual' period of traditional BMW evolutionary styling, rear-wheel drive M cars with a manual gearbox. The arrival of the Chris Bangle-styled BMWs heralded a discernible sea-change, and the advent of larger, more gadget packed mainstream models. *Car and Driver* magazine, for one, remains hopeful of a return to the smaller, more agile ways of the E39 5 Series, but, until that happens, there are always the classics.

Marc Cranswick

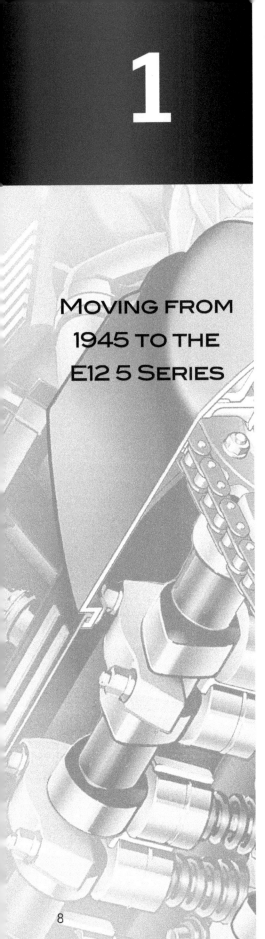

1

MOVING FROM 1945 TO THE E12 5 SERIES

The old Town Hall and Mint Grun 5 Series in mid '70s Weissenburg, Bavaria!
(Courtesy Fritz Lauterbach)

DIFFICULT BUSINESS TIMES

One cannot even begin to comprehend the base from which BMW rose after the end of the Second World War. The aeroplane engine factories in Munich and Berlin were destroyed, and its Eisenach plant was under Russian control. BMW's top engineers were in Britain as part of the reparation after the conflict.

BMW was forced to start over again, a practice it became accustomed to doing in the decades to come. In 1946, the Munich factory began manufacture of just about anything and everything, from whatever metal supplies existed: pots, pans, bicycles, and even farm equipment.

Momentum soon built up and production moved on to include motorcycles, the first reminder of BMW's prewar excellence. The Bavarian company had achieved fame in motorcycle production and competition but, in subsequent years, there occurred what can only be described as a marketing error. BMW engaged in the development

A 1972 BMW R75/5, accompanied by a Velorex sidecar; examples of BMW's motorcycle tradition.
(Courtesy Hans Vaalund)

Okay, the class competitive 520 twin carb pictured at Munich's Nymphenburg Castle, was no ball of fire. However, swifter E12s were on the way. (Courtesy *WHEELS*)

BMWs were designed to lean into corners. Bob Bondurant said that they only lean so far, then stick like glue! (Courtesy BMW)

of a luxurious saloon that came to be known as the Baroque Putto, because of its dumpy shape. Whilst the BMW 501/502 was a fine automobile, encompassing an innovative, all-aluminium V8 engine designed by Alfred Boning, it just didn't put food on the BMW table. The 501/2, and various spin-off

models like the 507 coupé styled by Count Albrecht Goertz and owned by Elvis Presley, whilst great image builders, resulted in BMW being dangerously compromised financially.

To keep matters in check BMW acquired the rights to make the Italian designed Isetta or "bubble

The E12 was on sale in Japan and Australia, from 1974! (Courtesy BMW)

The BMW Dixi (Austin 7) and Bubblecar (Isetta), were stepping stones to the E12 5 Series. (Courtesy Greg Johnson)

Gradual evolution in styling and engineering. The new '73 MY 520i, shown here, had a revised version of the 2000tii's 130bhp motor. (Courtesy Ulrich Thieme)

BMW's luxury cars cost too much to make and didn't sell in sufficient numbers, that was the bottom line. It wasn't long before the small German car maker became the subject of takeover bids from American Motors, the Rootes Group and, most worryingly, Daimler-Benz. American Motors and the Rootes Group were looking for beachheads into the Continental European market. These two companies and Daimler-Benz were both unsuccessful in their takeover bids.

It has been well documented how shareholder solidarity, most notably represented by the Quandt family, beat off all takeover proposals and saved

car". In the difficult years after the war, the German people needed cost effective, basic transportation. The Isetta and cars like Hans Glas's Goggomobil satisfied initial demands for low cost vehicles that could be operated with a cheaper motorcycle license and still offer some of the convenience and practicality of a regular car. This was all well and good at first, but it wasn't long before the German public, and other buyers in Europe, craved a more refined, developed small family car. The Isetta did its best to keep BMW afloat and racked up a not inconsiderable 162,000 units by the end of production in 1962.

The problem was that BMW had covered the top and bottom ends of the car market with not much in-between. A V8 limousine, with designer siblings, plus what amounted to an adapted three-wheeler, just wasn't what the market wanted. The cars that were wanted were the Fiat 500, Mini and VW Beetle: real small, cost-effective

family transportation. They spelt the end of the motorcycle-related bubblecar and microcar era. By May 1957, BMW was charging one thousand US dollars more for its six-pot 501 than the Mercedes 220S.

Writing for *WHEELS* magazine in March 1973, Jerry Sloniger said, "When this machine was originally introduced late last year I admired the way it moved around the company test track."[1]

---

1. Footnote (2) WHEELS, March 1973 p36

The 02 family notched up over 800,000 sales, helping to put BMW in the driver's seat.
(Courtesy Robert Styperek)

the day, buying time for BMW's development team to finish the life-saving 1500 Neue Klasse car of 1961/2; the rest, as they say, is history! After years of struggle the tide had turned, marking the start of better days for BMW. The company was now in control of its own destiny and free to exploit the lucrative middle ground that had eluded it for so long. As part of economic restructuring, BMW obtained a $12.5 million loan from the Bavarian state government. These funds helped develop the BMW 1500-2000, and subsequent related '02, families.

Under the guidance of salesman extraordinaire Paul Hahnemann, the lucrative market made up of affluent German middle class citizens was there for the taking. The new 1500 was all about exploiting niche markets, fulfilling a demand for a quality, sporty saloon, superior to commonplace Opels and German Fords, but not quite in Daimler-Benz territory. After years in the marketing wilderness BMW had come in from the cold. Production of the V8/microcar brigade would soon be curtailed or stopped altogether to free up production capacity for the new saloons. The future lay with the 1500, 1600 and 1800 models, so, wisely, that's where the emphasis was placed.

BMW's phoenix-like rise in the next decade was, as some have described, a jewel in the Wirtschaftswunder, or successful postwar reconstruction of German industry. The 1500/1800, and truncated 1600-2, accelerated the run along the path to the pot of gold. In 1966 the 02's launch party occurred during the celebrations of BMW's 50th birthday party held at the Bavarian State Opera House. It was the year BMW's annual production topped 60,000 units for the first time. It also represented the first year that BMW seriously got involved with exports, marked by the launch of the 2000CS coupé.

BMW needed extra production capacity to create the Neue Klasse family of automobiles that people wanted. To this end, 1966 also saw BMW acquire Glas, the company formed by fifties technical pioneer Hans Glas. Of greater importance was the ultra modern Dingolfing factory that came with the purchase, a great place to build the future 5 Series! By the late sixties, BMW was fit enough to have a crack at arch rival Daimler-Benz. The successful four-cylinder cars created enough surplus cash for the development of high class six-cylinder saloons and coupés.

The 2500/2800 saloon and 2800CS coupé, known internally

The owner's handbook for the very first 5 Series. (Courtesy BMW)

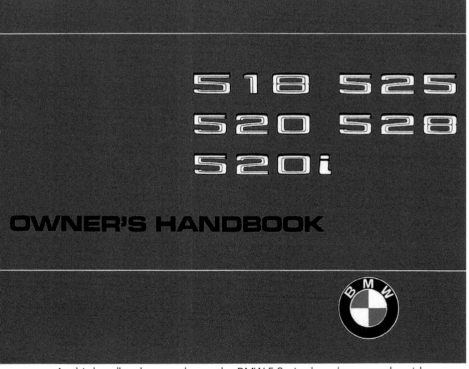

As this handbook cover shows, the BMW 5 Series has always used a wide range of the company's engines. (Courtesy BMW)

as the E3 and E9 respectively, represented the brave new front. The new, upscale cars would take the battle directly to equivalent engined Daimler-Benz models, the MB 250/280S class saloons and 280SL coupé, which had recently received a larger engine. Unlike the BMW 501/2 and its relations, these expensive newcomers proved commercially successful and took BMW into the mid to late seventies.

BMW'S BIG COMEBACK
In 1971 BMW could proudly state that it was currently moving more petrol-engined cars than Daimler-Benz managed in 1969. This may sound like left-handed praise, but remember that BMW was nearly flat on its corporate back just a few years earlier, and didn't look like it was even going to make it to fifty independently. By 1976, annual production was up to 275,000 units; by 1978 it was 320,000 and, in 1980, it scaled 350,000! In 1985, Jean Lindamood noted, when writing for *Car and Driver* (*C&D*), that only BMW could claim to have increased sales in North America in each successive year between 1974 and 1985.

So BMW had a great time from 1962 to 1972, but what then? It would just have to do it all over again for the seventies! The 1972 5 Series, codenamed E12, would help in achieving this goal. The 1500/2000 range and 02 models had made money for BMW, but it's no secret that development of an all new model involves a great deal of financial strain, especially true for a small outfit. BMW would eventually spend more money designing the 1992 BMW E36 3 Series' dashboard, than Rolls-

Royce spent on developing the entire new 1981 Silver Spirit. Little wonder, then, that the Bavarians subsequently bought the Crewe concern, lock, stock and two smoking barrels!

The development of the late sixties luxury saloon and coupé, together with introduction in the early seventies of the 5 Series, really forced BMW to dig deep into the pockets of its business suit. The new 5 just had to do well, even better than well, to offset the outlay and keep BMW on track. *Management Today* summed it up by saying that, whilst it would be overkill to say that the 1500/2000 successor would alone determine if BMW ran out the seventies as an independent company, the new model would demonstrate whether BMW was still on the winning path it had taken so long to find.

Some would cite the BMW 02 and subsequent 3 Series as the cars that put BMW on the map. However, as stated by economist, John Maynard Keynes, we are all dead in the long run! The 3 Series may have turned out the greatest thing since sliced bread, but success in business is cumulative. Failure with the 1972 5 Series would have resulted in insufficient funds to make the 3 Series as good a car as it indeed turned out to be. In other words, short run problems can damage the commercial success of future models.

BMW was always bullish, even in the midst of adversity. In the 1960s, its super salesman 'Niche' Paul Hahnemann dismissed Mercedes as producing, "cars for rich, careful grandpas."[2] By mid 1969, BMW's marketing director, H.W.

2. *Management Today, January 1971 p49*

Bonsch, stated that the world knew Mercedes invented the motorcar, but that BMW wanted to give the successful businessman a choice.

Bonsch added, "If he likes to drive and wants performance more than he wants the Mercedes name he'll buy a BMW. Mercedes is living off its reputation." The quote was given to Patrick Bedard in a report on the new E3 2500. It was printed, in the June 1969 issue of *Car and Driver*.

In a 1974 follow up to its initial look at the diminutive Bavarian, *Managament Today* noted that the initial 520 and 525 were instant hits! Pretty much the same happened when the 3, 6 and 7 Series cars arrived. What made the quick success of the newcomers even more remarkable was the limited advertising and public awareness of BMW cars outside West Germany. Television commercials and magazine spreads were commonplace at home, but quite limited in export markets compared to today. The good commercial performance of the seventies newcomers allowed BMW to build up funds once again and plough them back into research and development (R&D) to create great new models for the years to come.

So what exactly was a 5 Series? Quite simply, the successor to the company-saving 1500/2000 range of the sixties. Known internally as the E12, some feel its name is derived from the fact it was the fifth new class model range after the important 1500. With the 1500/2000, 02, 2500/2800 saloons and 2800/3.0CS coupés, it does indeed make the 1972 5 Series number five. Others consider the model tag to be a simple amalgam

of seating capacity and metric motor capacity.

The E12 became the first regular production BMW to benefit from the touch of BMW's new head of styling Paul Bracq. The Frenchman replaced Wilhelm Hoftmeister and the 5 Series was the first mainstream work done for BMW after Bracq's 1972 Turbo show car. Bracq had just come from Daimler-Benz, where he had done the styling on all the contemporary models. The inspiration for the E12 came from the BMW 2000 TI Bertone styling exercise known as Garmisch. Bertone had created a coupé that was exhibited at Geneva 1970.

It's felt by some that the coupé inspiration compromised the styling balance of what was to be a four-door car, although some coachbuilders did do custom estate conversions. The majority of folks judged the new E12 to be a modern, conservative but attractive successor to the 1500/2000, even if some home market buyers felt that contemporary German cars had a little too much US influence in their appearance. In the sixties, the US Corvair compact had an impact on the styling of several cars, including BMW's line-up.

For the seventies the BMW C pillar and tall greenhouse were blended into the contemporary wedge shape. The 5 Series had a profile that gradually fell from the boot to the bonnet. More overt exponents of the wedge theme were the Triumph TR7 and Alfa GTV. *Road & Track* (*R&T*) noted that the new Fox-bodied 1979 Mustang had the same flat planes, creases and styling cues evidenced by the original 5 Series BMW. The magazine also mentioned that such a look had become a fad.

The early four-cylinder 520i was a sporty car, that matched the go of the 1974-76 525 twin carb. 5 Series production began at BMW's main Munich plant. It then moved to a new Dingolfing factory, finished in 1973, and by 1975 the transition was complete! (Courtesy Ulrich Thieme)

Commercial failure of the E12 would have compromised development of the original 3 Series.

NEW ENGINEERING

The 5 Series, as the 520 and 520i, were launched just after the close of the 1972 Munich Olympic Games. These were almost equivalent engined big brothers to the 2002 and 2002tii, but, in essence, were new from the ground up. Like their predecessors, they had steel unibody, MacPherson struts at the front and semi trailing arms at the rear. However, there were evolutionary improvements. The shell was more rigid, suspension travel was increased,

Between 1972 and 1975, the 520i used high pressure Kugelfischer mechanical fuel-injection. It was accurate, expensive and needed fine adjustment. (Courtesy Ulrich Thieme)

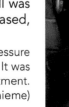

The 02's tall greenhouse and low belt line foretold BMW practice for years to come. (Courtesy Robert Styperek)

After designing the styling of all of Daimler-Benz's contemporary models, Paul Bracq built on the earlier work of Wilhelm Hoftmeister at BMW. The E12 was the first production car he designed for his new employer. (Courtesy Lee Wareham)

Paul Bracq's modern, but conservative,
E12 styling involved fashionable short
rear deck and slight wedge profile.
(Courtesy Ulrich Thieme)

The E12's safety dash had draught
free flow through ventilation. Early
cars had contrasting gray vent grilles.
(Courtesy Ulrich Thieme)

and a revised ZF steering gear possessed more 'feel' but required less muscle. The radiator was rubber rather than rigidly mounted, and the rear spring/shocks were mounted together, which allowed the fitting of the Boge 'Nivomat' self-leveling rear suspension, as seen on the larger E3 2500/2800.

The new body structure weighed 110 pounds more than a similarly equipped 2000, and with good reason. The E12, unlike its exclusively four-cylinder predecessor, was designed to accommodate BMW's M30 big six. The extra four inches in length

allowed the engineers to shoehorn BMW's largest motor into the new mid ranger. It was all part of BMW's plan to compete with Daimler-Benz's successful W114 compact. Both the W114 and BMW's E12 were styled by Paul Bracq, and both had rear deck fuel fillers until the mid to late seventies.

It wasn't long before there was a similar engined petrol powered 5 Series for each Daimler-Benz compact. This explained the initial absence of a 518. Whilst the 1800 had been the biggest seller in BMW's old range, there was no MB 180, so BMW didn't create a 518,

until the 1973/4 fuel crisis sparked increased interest in smaller engined thrifty mobiles! Even so soon after near bankruptcy BMW couldn't help itself from harrassing the Prussian automaker. The E12 and W114 were so similar that even *Managament Today* referred to the four-cylinder E12 as the 520 compact!

Of course, BMW didn't offer any diesels in its range – but the night was yet young! The point had already been made that the Bavarian concern was taking its new mid ranger upmarket, taking the fight directly to Daimler-

By 1974 BMW had backtracked and introduced a 100mph 518 – a belated 1800 successor. (Courtesy Christian Hartmann)

The thrifty 90bhp single carb 1.8-litre, made the early 518 the only E12 with a manual choke. It was also the only E12 not needing 98 octane fuel. (Courtesy Christian Hartmann)

Benz, and if Daimler-Benz could offer air-conditioning, so too could BMW. The E12's dashboard was an energy absorbing, high quality plastic moulding featuring numerous ventilation outlets. The old vent wings were eliminated, their role taken over by the ample, fan-assisted, stratified fresh air and heating equipment.

The original 5 Series was the first medium sized bimmer to have factory fitted, Behr designed air-con. Dash instrumentation was typically BMW sparse. In the raised instrument binnacle were equally oversized speedo and rev counters, flanked by smaller, but also circular, temperature and fuel gauges. Other information on the car's vital life signs came from differently lit tell-tale lamps. The whole scenario was in complete contrast to the sixties performance car image of banks of circular gauges. *R&T* stated that BMW engineers looked forward to a time when technology had advanced to the stage where the driver received audible warnings.

All-in-all the original 5 Series displayed the thoroughness and attention to detail that the world has come to expect from BMW. In fact, a rechargeable torch in the glovebox, as per Daimler-Benz's 1971 MB 350SL, was proof that the only thing that the new BMW 5 was devoid of was compromise!

Product placement saw an unmarked E12 520 being used by German TV Chief Inspector Derrick in 1974.
(Courtesy Christian Hartmann)

A 1979 BMW 520/6 with 16in Alpina rims, five-speed stick shift, Alpina steering wheel and ASS Scheel bucket seats.
(Courtesy Friedrich Schroeder)

2

EXPORTS AHOY! BMW ATTACKS THE US MARKET

BMW 520. Konsequenz sportlicher Vernunft

JOINING THE 2002 & 3.0SI

As BMW acquired a worldwide reputation for creating quality sports saloons very early in its history, it is surprising how late it was in the West German Wirtschaftswunder that BMW started seriously exporting its products, since this is of prime importance once a car maker has achieved saturation point in the local market. Back in 1971, export chief Hermann Winkler noted that the US market was too volatile to rely on for more than ten per cent of BMW's export business. This strategy was in contrast to other European producers, who were rushing full throttle into the large and potentially profitable North American market.

North America was, and still is, a key market for the sale of automobiles. In fact, *CAR* noted in August 1984 that Jaguar, Daimler-Benz and BMW refused to reveal the proportion of profits derived from that single market. *CAR* stated that, in the case of Jaguar, the figure could have been as high as seventy per cent. In short, it was a market that no international car maker could afford to ignore.

What can be said about North America and BMW? It's correct to say that BMWs were sold in the US from a very early date, but not in so many numbers that one would notice. In the fifties, a trickle of Baroque Putto saloons, and mechanically related vehicles like the 507 V8, made their way across the water to wealthy patrons. However, the sales volume was very small and, as stated earlier, even extravagant pricing couldn't help BMW turn a profit on the V8 luxury sports car line.

Once again it was BMW's sixties achievements that paved the way for the success it enjoys today in America and the rest of the world. At $2613 list price, the 1967 BMW 1600-2 had 95% of a 200 horse Mustang 289's performance, at a lower price. Combining the quality of larger, more expensive BMWs, with affordability and even sportier size, it was an offer the US enthusiast couldn't refuse. Then came the 1968 BMW 2002. From this point on, US buyer interest blossomed; the floodgates opened at long last. North American buyers became acquainted with BMW offerings bearing the blue and white roundel – just in time!

The 5 Series arrived in the US in the midst of major changes in the American automotive scene. What had held true for as long as anyone could remember was just

Road & Track was correct to speculate that BMW wouldn't export the four-cylinder 520/520i to America, due to range rationalisation. (Courtesy Peter Kilner & Peter Hackney, http://team-orange.blogspot.com/)

A Volvo 240 in hot pursuit! The E12 520i started out competing with the, also German injected, Volvo 144E. (Courtesy Peter Kilner & Peter Hackney, http://team-orange.blogspot.com/)

Traditional BMW New Class sporting qualities, in a slightly larger and more refined form.
(Courtesy Peter Kilner & Peter Hackney, http://team-orange.blogspot.com/)

The four-cylinder powered E12s weren't as prone to oversteer as the M30-powered editions.
(Courtesy Peter Kilner & Peter Hackney, http://team-orange.blogspot.com/)

This Swedish 1976 525 has the optional rear head restraints and 6.5x14-inch turbine alloy rims, rather than the more common 6x14-inch version. (Courtesy Niklas Edlund)

722,435 E 12 5 Series were made, covering manufacture & CKD in West Germany, South Africa, Thailand, Indonesia, Uruguay and Portugal during 1972-85. (Courtesy Niklas Edlund)

plain gone, and nothing would ever be quite the same again. The homeland of the automobile for the masses, where cheap gasoline and big production runs made car ownership possible for more, sooner, was going through unprecedented change.

After the Second World War, Mr and Mrs Average were presented with larger, more powerful and lavishly equipped cars at relatively reasonable prices. With annual production of popular models easily running into tens of thousands, Detroit was very much the motor city. In such a large and lucrative market, an optimist could cling to the hope that American Motors could stake a solid claim as America's fourth largest player.

By the early seventies, the US scene had evolved into three layers. At the top of the tree was the full-size car, the area where the majority of design resources had been directed. These vehicles measured between 210 and 230 inches in length and were supposed to be able to carry six

people. Below this group lay the intermediates at around 10 inches shorter and slightly narrower. They had grown in popularity with those buyers not requiring the full measure of space, or not desiring the bigger sticker price of the larger cars. Finally, there were the compacts, and – within this class – the increasingly popular subcompacts. Cars measuring between 170 and 195 inches fell into this group.

Compact cars had grown in popularity since the fifties, when European cars, most noticeably the VW Beetle, demonstrated that US buyers wanted another option to the established Detroit menu selection. Worried about market share taken by foreign makes, Detroit launched its take on the compact idea with the Chevy Corvair, Ford Falcon and Chrysler Valiant as the sixties dawned.

As time went on, it became apparent that US buyers wanted the virtues of small cars at the top end of town, too. From the late sixties, European imports like

the Daimler-Benz compact, Audi/NSU 100, Volvo 144, Peugeot 504 and Saab 99 had some success in enticing buyers away from a bedecked intermediate. They were something of a conundrum for US buyers in that they avoided the harsh ride, spartan, economy image of similarly sized domestic compacts, and combined this with a price tag more in keeping with a larger lavish car.

It was at this expensive compact class that BMW was pitching its US 5 Series. The E3 2500/2800 cars had already been introduced, and had done reasonably good trade, at least once BMW priced the car more competitively and renamed it the Bavaria for 1971. As things stood, a correctly specified US E12 would nicely fill the yawning gap between the US 2002 and the big ticket 3.0 Si E3 luxo saloon. Whilst a US 5 Series was just what the doctor ordered, it was still a question of timing. The 1973/4 fuel crisis, the arrival of stricter pollution controls, and Federal dictates about auto safety

Emergency services in West Germany made use of the Porsche 924 and BMW E12 5 Series. A 1978 520 is shown here.
(Courtesy Ulrich Thieme)

A fire brigade BMW 520, alongside the E12's predecessor, a series 2 (post 1967) BMW 2000 Automatic. (Courtesy Ulrich Thieme)

E12s were used by the police force and ambulance service. The British police force also used E12s in the '70s. (Courtesy Ulrich Thieme)

The low set E12 dashboard allowed for auxiliary equipment to be fitted, but form certainly followed function! (Courtesy Ulrich Thieme)

Special order emergency service E12s had a very spartan, 518 style, vinyl-trimmed interior. (Courtesy Ulrich Thieme)

By 1978 regular 520s had switched to the new 2-litre M60 baby six. However, this fire brigade 520 was still using the twin carb M10. (Courtesy Ulrich Thieme)

meant that the cosy US car scene described above was getting all shook up!

In light of this turbulent automotive state, BMW decided to sit it out for a moment. It had seen how many imports had tripped over the changing conditions and Federal directives of the early seventies. It made sense to spend extra time developing a 5 Series appropriate for North America.

So it was that buyers had to wait until the 1975 model year before the E12, in the form of the US 530i, ventured Stateside, and not a moment too soon. For various reasons, such as imminent model replacement, proposed safety laws, and tightened emissions regulations, the US bimmer model line-up had been severely pruned.

Looking at the 1975 model year, and leaving out the new US 530i, BMW had just two variants on offer: the single carb 2002 and the top echelon 3.0Si; the Karmann-built CS coupé had been bidden farewell at the close of the 1974 model year. To make matters worse the 3.0Si was getting ready to pack up and leave at the close of the 1976 model year. The pressure was on the US E12 to make a big splash! Beyond the 530i, there were other new considerations for 1975 regarding BMW and North America.

First off there was BMW North America itself. It was the first time that BMW had set up shop in the States and handled the import distribution business personally. Up

As early as 1974/5 European buyers were already spoilt for choice. The car pictured has the flat bonnet pressing used by four-cylinder E12s up to 1977. (Courtesy BMW)

First shown at the 1973 Frankfurt Motor Show, the 1974 BMW 525 had a de-tuned 145hp version of the E3 2500's M30 I6. (Courtesy Christian Hartmann)

The 525, and subsequent 1975 528 companion, were soft tune executive E12s compared to the rorty 520i. (Courtesy Christian Hartmann)

At controls like these, *Autocar* magazine (UK) got 117mph and 0-60mph in 10.6 seconds with its 525. The journal's equivalent 520i figures were 114mph and 10.5 seconds. (Courtesy Christian Hartmann)

In 1974, German tuner Gerhard Schnedier's 525-based GS Tuning 530 could do 0-60mph in a little over 6 seconds, and reach almost 150mph! (Courtesy Christian Hartmann)

Actress Hidemi Aoki with a 1976 tuner MSM 528 3.5. (Courtesy www.nepoeht.com)

It was ironic that the racing CSL was used to promote the new 530i, given that it was based on the CS coupé that had been discontinued in the US at the close of the 1974 model year. (Courtesy Tod Bryant)

until then, Max Hoffman's company had handled the import and sale of bimmers in North America, seeing business grow from a trickle to 15,000 cars a year by the close of the 1974 model year. It made sense for BMW to step in at this point, and the new head quarters was in Montvale New Jersey.

BMW was also getting into local racing circles, taking its racing CSL coupés away from the hurly-burly of the European Touring Car Championships for a tour of duty in the United States' local International Motor Sports Association, or IMSA, racing series. BMW fielded a two car team comprising Hans Stuck jr, Ronnie Peterson and Brian Redman with Sam Posey. There was some irony in using the CSL coupé to raise interest in the States regarding the new 530i, since the US CS coupé

North America did get a 5 Series of its very own – the Federalised 1975 530i. (Courtesy BMW)

Complying with 1975 US emissions regulations without a catalytic converter called for some lateral thinking: the 1975 US 530i produced 176bhp net using leaded regular. (Courtesy BMW)

had been axed at the end of 1974! As early 530is hit showrooms, the two car racing team went about its business on east coast tracks such as Daytona and Watkins Glen, and west coast tracks such as Monterey, Riverside, Laguna Seca and Sebring.

BMW needed the PR shot in the arm that IMSA racing could deliver. Whilst it's true that Jackie Onassis owned a 1974 3.0S, and the 2002 had worked up quite a following among hard core enthusiasts by this stage, North America at large still didn't know what a bimmer was. *R&T* noted that, back in the late sixties, most Americans would guess that BMW stood for British Motor Works! So it comes as

no surprise that a number of US newspapers printed exactly this mistake when writing about BMW's entry into IMSA exploits. BMW responded by plastering 'Bavarian Motor Works' in large letters at the top of the racing CSLs' windshields, just in case!

So, what was a 530i? Basically, the European 525 of 1973 fitted with a detoxed 3-litre version of BMW's M30 big six, topped off with Bosch electronic L – jetronic fuel-injection. The 530i was offered in both manual and automatic forms, with a luxurious level of trim not frequently encountered on European variants. While European BMWs were still well entrenched in the era of everything being

optional, except the steering wheel, concessions were made to the competitive nature of the US auto arena. Thus, the 530i came with a tach, map pockets, full wood trim, front head restraints and a lockable glovebox.

Given that the US 530i was priced as high as a Caddy, it would have been crazy to walk in wearing anything less. 530is, like the contemporary European 528 range topper, had power steering as standard. This was necessary, given that such cars came with 6-inch wide rims and 195/70 rubber, otherwise the steering would be too heavy when parking. Dealers often ordered cars with air-conditioning and a radio, making it

BMW's 500 SERIES—THEY KEEP GETTING BETTER..

528

WHAT DIFFERENCE can 300cc make? In the case of BMW's 500-series cars, it can make a whole world of difference. Fitting the 2.8-litre six to the 525 has transformed it from a performance sedan to a supremely comfortable *high* performance machine, rivalling even the bigger models in the BMW range for handling and power, and providing value for money — or so Matt Whelan would have you believe . . .

The Euro E12 528 twin carb, was BMW's performance benchmark, when creating the US spec 1975 530i. That is, 0-60mph in 9 seconds and a 124mph top speed. (Courtesy *Modern Motor*)

virtually impossible to find a plain vanilla 530i at the base sticker price. Still, that was the way people ordered their cars, so it made sense to have showroom cars equipped to that specification.

Both *R&T* and *C&D* tested factory air conditioned 530is with four-speed stick shifts in the middle of 1975. *C&D*'s rival comparison table is interesting because of the diversity of models the US 530i might come up against, plus the performance figures achievable through diverse technical approaches. The 530i as tested cost more, accelerated faster, registered more decibels and braked from 70mph in a shorter distance than did the Cadillac Sedan DeVille. The bimmer also had better gas mileage; hardly surprising when you consider that the BMW motor was 5.2 litres smaller!

Another example of automotive divergence came with the offering of manual transmission. It wasn't common in the US then or now, certainly not in the expensive saloon class. Sure, buyers in the pony car scene liked four on the floor, or – to a lesser degree – three on the tree, but on a luxury four-door? That was heresy in the States! An expensive luxo barge was the last place you would find a stick. *R&T* said as much in 1972 when it did a group shakedown of the Jaguar XJ6, Mercedes 280 and BMW 3.0S. It commented that all three could be had as manuals in their home markets, but in the States it was strictly autopilot, except for the 3.0S.

US buyers did purchase more than a few manual BMWs: the order rate for stick shift 3.0Sis was nearly 50%; for the 530i, according to an *R&T* owner survey, the figure was 70%. A contemporary market commentator would have said that offering a standard shift in this neck of the woods made little sense. The fact is that BMW offered a manual and buyers did choose it. It was the availability of the manual that put greater distance between

The 530i shared its L-jetronic, 3-litre inline 6 with the contemporary US market 3.0Si; it was rated at 176 horsepower net. Claus Luthe oversaw the 1977 E12 restyle. (Courtesy David Scott)

BMW and its competitors in the States. Patrick Bedard for one was glad of the free market approach. He mentioned that Daimler-Benz saw fit to offer manual labour with its base economy 240D only. The 530i proved that interest in the U shift device still existed.

In an holistic sense, both *R&T* and *C&D* were pleased with the German newbie. However, opinion differed on the suspension. *R&T* proclaimed that it was supple in the extreme without slop, *C&D* made it clear it wanted firmer suspenders. It would be fair to say that 1975 and 1976 BMWs tended to have soft suspension settings. This quality wasn't restricted to US bimmers: when *Autocar* tested the BMW 316 in January 1976, it noted that the car had unusually soft suspension.

The first 3 and 5 Series models did have greater suspension travel than their predecessors, and it made sense to take advantage of this quality. Softer hardware would deliver improved ride comfort without noticeably adverse consequences for handling, at least for the majority of BMW's ever-widening audience. The move to go soft may also have been a conscious decision to please US tastes. Early Jaguar XJ6 and XKE cars had overly light power steering.

Consumer Union noted in 1970 that the new-to-America Audi 100 had very soft suspension for an import. Foreign manufacturers were trying to establish what it was that North America wanted from their cars, and matters went too far with regard to comfort. BMW went even softer with 5 Series suspension in 1978-79, before going noticeably

firmer for 1980. *Autocar* even reversed its opinion on the BMW 316 in January 1982, saying the ride had become borderline harsh!

If it was all-change on the suspension front, things remained pretty much constant in the engine room. BMW's contemporary motors had drawn praise from around the world, and the US was no exception. *R&T* staff considered the 3-litre six the best of its layout. With the intensification of pollution controls, driveability had become of prime importance in the US. *R&T* was pro fuel-injection for maintaining driveability in a scenario of tightening emissions regulations, and not afraid to make its views known on more than one occasion.

So, the 530i was considered a good bet by *R&T*, because the electronic injection, twin thermal reactor and leaded fuel route facilitated the creation of a beast that could start easily, be driven away immediately and pull a tall gear with very few rpm on the tach. In this case, a gear as high as fourth and with as little as 1000rpm dialled in. A great achievement given the compromises engineers were forced to make in those challenging times. Colourful *C&D* simply said that the motor allowed roadside telephone poles to be placed behind one expeditiously.

Both *R&T* and *C&D* were pleased with the 530i's interior ambiance, possessing, as it did, high quality materials presented in a tasteful, restrained fashion and accompanied by thoughtfully placed controls and instruments. In short, everything was where it should be to get on with the serious business of safe, continuous high speed travel. The best feature in the interior? That would have to be the stick shift; tester consensus was that this was the only way to specify your new US 530i. Choose the auto and you would be selling the whole deal short.

Since 1972's introduction of the 3-litre M30 six, BMW had started using Getrag synchronisers in place of the previous Borg-Warner offerings. The old ZF four-speeders had a real light action, but they had weak synchros that were just not up to the challenge of dealing with the larger displacement 3-litre. *R&T* commented that, with the new box, the synchronisers couldn't be beaten, but there remained the BMW bugbear of a noisy clutch throwout bearing, and the shifter action was a touch notchy. Initially, the 1975 1/2 530i shared the 3.0Si's BW65 3-speed auto. Although better than the pre

'72 ZF autoboxes of E3/E9s, mid '76 MY saw the super ZF 3HP 22. This new design moved from old fashioned brake bands to clutches.

If anything the 530i made things tough for the US 6 series when it came over in 1977. The E24 6 series was based on the 5 Series; given that the US version would share its engine and gearbox with the US 530i, it's no wonder that value comparisons were made. In Europe – where buyers were less likely to make value-for-cash comparisons, and it would be less likely to find similarly specified 5 and 6 series cars – the issue didn't arise. In Europe both cars sold to an even smaller band of customers, and were far enough apart in market segment that similarities in driving experience didn't raise questions of duplication.

In May 1977 the US 530i and 630CSi had base sticker prices of $12,495 and $23,600 respectively: one heck of a difference for similarly designed and powered vehicles. Conservative *R&T* was moved to say "But we're left with one nagging thought. A 530i doesn't give up much to a 630CSi, has four doors, comfortable seating for four (or a friendly five) and costs about half as much. Whether the coupé's distinctive styling and slightly better overall performance are worth an extra $11,000 is something only your ego and your pocketbook can decide".

C&D didn't mince its words and was much more direct about the form in which the US 6 series landed in North America and its pricing strategy. It said it needed more 'moxie' [power] to do the deed against the Jaguar XJS and the Mercedes 450SLC. Indeed, *C&D* went to great lengths to state

that, whilst it admired shoe box bimmers, somehow the coupés just seemed to come up short. Objectively, there is no doubt that the 630CSi had its work cut out trying to match the larger engined British and German cars. Perhaps one can say that, whilst BMW saloons surprised many with its sports car character, the coupés displeased some because they were too much like saloons.

Still, if the 630CSi was more boulevard than bestial, did it really matter? North America was experiencing big change in its automotive value system. Mies van der Rohe, when commenting on the over-ornamentation of 19th century architecture, said that less is more. Traditionally, US buyers were used to getting their automotive pound of flesh, but, with all the pressures of pollution control, economy constraints and different buyer tastes, the status quo was changing.

The postwar idyll was an imposing chromium radiator grille adorned with stylised crest, pinstriping, fake wire wheel covers on whitewalls and half vinyl covered roof. On the inside a myriad of convenience features accompanied by US boudoir style trimmings. Put a Johnny Mathis cartridge in the 8 track player, dial in the desired temperature setting on the climate control a/c, snick the column shifter into drive and enjoy whisper quiet, undisturbed turnpike cruising.

Many buyers still wanted traditional style cars. Time and time again buyers rushed back to first full-size and subsequently larger cars when fuel prices eased. Demand stayed stable in trying times and improved with the

In keeping with all US bimmers between 1975 and the start of 1979, the 530i utilised a leaded regular/thermal reactor approach to meet emissions regulations. Non-Californian 530is had advanced ignition timing giving better gas mileage and engine response. (Courtesy David Scott)

merest movement of the storm clouds. In 1985, a decade later, Ford said it would stick with rear drive for its full-size line due to buyer dictates. Off course, the success of GM's downsized large cars indicated that, although US buyers still wanted and needed big cars, they preferred better designed large cars.

There were also many who found Detroit's redesigned large cars still too big for their liking. They had been exposed to European style sports luxury models, like the BMW 530i, and found that the compromises such vehicles made were closer to the type of car they wanted. There was an appreciation of the 530i's compact, understated and manoeuvrable take on the luxury concept. For an increasing number of Stateside buyers, this was where they spent their disposable income in the years ahead.

Hold on, though, don't throw away your tailfins just yet! It should be noted that European imports had their problems in the early years. Their small displacement motors didn't handle an autobox with aplomb, overheating was common, and air-conditioning systems were often inadequate. Plus, the scanty dealer servicing network, which often concentrated on the east and west coasts with precious little in-between, made breakdowns and parts ordering a

The US 528i of 1979 was the first BMW to use the 3-way catalytic converter/unleaded fuel emissions system which is taken for granted on the majority of vehicles today. (Courtesy Adam Wilson)

The stick shift US 528i made 169bhp on expensive 91 octane unleaded gasoline: independent magazine tests put its 0 to 60 time at a touch over 8 seconds. (Courtesy Adam Wilson)

real headache for many. So buying a European import was still an expensive gamble, even as late as the mid seventies. A well specified US intermediate would have been a wiser choice in terms of practical everyday use and reliability than something like an imported Citroën DS.

R&T wasn't joking when it made the following comment regarding the BMW Bavaria saloons and related coupés: "When BMW engineers designed their cars in the '60s and '70s, apparently they had in mind cool breezes wafting through Bavarian forests, not the sizzling summertime temperatures of the US." Needless to say, BMW and other European manufacturers quickly resolved problem areas and came up with models better suited to wider climatic variations.

Beyond this there was still the issue of value for money. Patrick Bedard contrasted what he called the "Persian pleasure domes" of Detroit with the new age functionalism of the BMW 530i. He noted that most Americans were of the opinion that the bimmer's interior didn't reflect what it cost, but countered that with "If you think that tinsel and velvet interiors look expensive, BMW is just independent enough to consider that your problem". Even so, many were left pondering why it cost quite so much just to get a margin of greater functionalism.

Rich Ceppos said as much in June 1980 when comparing the BMW 733i with the Pontiac Bonneville. The 733i seated one less person, had an EPA rating 2mpg lower, cost a massive $21,971 more ... and you had to still change gear yourself! Ceppos said that, to a typical Bonneville man, paying 30 grand for a car you had to shift yourself must have seemed as dumb as buying land by mail!

As far as improving on the value for money picture, BMW did increase the level of standard equipment for its US versions as the years went by. By 1978 the 530i had air-conditioning and power windows as standard equipment.

This 700bhp, 1980 528i Turbo has a dual 3-inch stainless steel Mandrel bend side exhaust, and was in the June 2006 issue of *Performance BMW*. (Courtesy Zane Coker & Max Earey)

A comfy seat of power, with E34 540i power and heated leather seats. The interior carries extra wood appliqué embellishments. (Courtesy Zane Coker and Max Earey)

This E26 M1-based block is a nitrous sniffing 4-litre, with Crower H-Beam billet rods. (Courtesy Zane Coker and *Performance BMW*)

As well as the turbo I6, some owners have sneaked in a Chevy LS1 V8 for quicker quarter-mile travel! (Courtesy Zane Coker & Max Earey)

had factory cruise as an option, but the US 530i didn't. If you wanted cruise it would have to be an aftermarket sourced and dealer fitted unit, like the one made by Escort.

Still, it was odd that the US 5 Series didn't have factory cruise or even optional power seats, features that were common by this stage on very humble domestic cars. Nobody ever said being rich was easy! With the first E12 5 series, exactly 27,870 US 530is were delivered to North American customers between 1975 and 1978. All things considered, the 530i had been pretty well received, neatly took over from the well known Bavaria, and gave something for US buyers to play with while BMW put the finishing touches to the Bavaria's real successor, the 1978 US 733i.

THE 530I BECOMES THE ECO FRIENDLY 528I

As far as US 5 Series models went the 530i passed the baton on to the new for 1979 US 528i. Like its European counterpart, the 528i, this model featured the 2.8-litre M30. In place of the 530i's leaded regular diet, air pump, exhaust gas recirculation and twin thermal reactors the 528i simplified matters by using just a three-way catalytic converter with Bosch lambda sond oxygen sensor, and a diet of unleaded fuel. In 1979 *C&D*, which gained initial fame for doing questionable comparisons like that between the Pontiac Catalina 2+2 and Ferrari 330/GT 2+2 in 1965, teamed up another automotive odd couple. 15 years later it was the US 528i and Pontiac Grand Am 301 that were locking metaphorical horns.

On the downside, BMW's decision not to fit an autosound system as part of the base sticker price didn't make many friends. The usual corporate line was that customers would wish to choose their own autosound system. However, this response was an insult to a buyer's intelligence when you could buy a tricked-out Trans Am for half the price of a BMW 530i. More than a few people were also miffed that cruise control wasn't part of the deal, either. The E12's successor

Back in 1969, the 7-litre Pontiac Grand Prix and BMW 2000 saloon were both available on the US market. However, the chance that both models would be considered by the same purchaser was remote to say the least. A decade on and such a comparison was no longer in the realms of fantasy. World fuel crises, pollution controls and fuel economy taxes, combined with shifting buyer tastes, had brought greater convergence between Detroit and Europe. European cars had grown and taken on more convenience features, whereas many familiar US cars had become trimmer of line and started to explore new directions.

So, for C&D's comparison we have the US 528i, a 2.8-litre six-cylinder saloon replete with standard air-con, power windows, mirror, power steering and other features that were never available on its sixties predecessor. In the red corner the Pontiac Grand Am, one of GM's new line of successful downsized intermediates. It featured a special lightweight 4.9-litre version of Pontiac division's medium block overhead valve V8, plus sports radial Rally Tuned Suspension, or RTS. In the words of C&D it was about the size of a contemporary Volvo 244 and had similar internal space. The Grand Am was GM's take on the increasingly popular European style sports saloon. Even if C&D said apples and oranges were being judged together, at least they were still comparing fruit!

Both cars were tuned to cope with 1979's pollution control and CAFE economy dictates. They both had motors with 8.2 to 1 compression, with catalytic converters, and running 91 octane

unleaded fuel. The 4.9-litre 301 V8 had been largely developed to cut weight and boost economy. When fitted to such diverse Pontiac models as the Bonneville, Grand Am, and even Trans Am, it would help maintain the fleet economy average and reduce the chances of incurring the dreaded gas guzzler tax. This it definitely achieved and C&D noted that both bimmer and Grand Am were EPA rated equal for city fuel consumption.

However, the economy drive compromised the Grand Am's ability to match the US 528i on performance. In spite of being a descendant of the 389 that powered the mighty GTO down the quarter mile, the 301's economy-focused single plane intake manifold, and small siamesed intake ports meant its 0 to 60 time of 9.9 seconds trailed the 528i's 8.3-second figure recorded in the same test. If the tables were turned with straight line performance, both cars stayed faithful to national origins in other respects.

The 528i, with its small displacement, high revving, electronically injected, six-cylinder motor with long intake runners, eked out every last drop of energy from the 91 octane fuel. It featured an easy-to-shift, floor-mounted four-speeder with a light clutch. At the back semi trailing arm independent rear suspension allowed European engineers to dial in a good compromise between handling and ride comfort. Four wheel disc brakes washed off excess speed at appropriate moments.

The Grand Am, while slimmed down, still had its fair share of Detroit DNA. The short stroke, cast iron, ohv V8, using a single four barrel

Rochester Quadrajet carb, relatively heavy action four-speed box, and solid rear axle, were all in evidence. Hardware that focused on durability and the ability to cope with a bucketload of torque from large displacement V8 motors obviously meant a different specification sheet to that of the 528i.

Then there was the small matter of price. The 528i was nearly double the Grand Am's price. Being a comparatively low volume, high priced car, it could use technical solutions that were just not economically feasible on more mainstream cars.

With this in mind, it's no surprise that the BMW's more sophisticated suspension allowed it to soak up the imperfections of Ohio's backroads where testing was done, with greater aplomb than the Pontiac. The BMW combined handling and a compliant ride to a greater degree than the Grand Am. The Pontiac under test had GM's Turbo Hydramatic autobox, well known for reliable and smooth shifting. GM's four-speed manual boxes, with their relatively heavy action and less than ideal pedal placement, were less impressive, and C&D noted that the test car benefited from a production difficulty that prevented a stick shift Grand Am being supplied.

It was the first year for the Grand Am with a catalytic converter and unleaded only; ditto for the bimmer. The US 528i was the world's most expensive lab rat, used to evaluate the switch to the three-way cat and unleaded diet before the US 3, 6 and 7 Series models were brought into line. There was only good news this time because the new emissions approach worked extremely well. *R&T* summed up matters best when it stated the following on its February 1979 528i test "A single 50 state version, with no EGR, no air injection and an ignition advance curve that allows it to run like God and Alex von Falkenhausen intended it to ..."

R&T recorded 0 to 60 in 8.2 seconds, a quarter mile in 16.7 seconds and a top speed of 125mph, some of the best figures for any car sold in emissions, CAFE-struck, late seventies America. They were better figures than the emissions compromised 530i could manage. If performance was improved, other items were much the same. Features that were still optional equipment were the two-way power roof, limited-slip differential, alloys, leather upholstery, metallic paint and a stereo! In the States you still couldn't get the optional firmer suspension available on European E12s.

BMW's corporate turbine alloys became standard for 1980. *C&D* noted on the eve of 1981 that, whilst the 528i's price was around 22 grand US, the US 5 Series still didn't have power seats, even as an option. The 5 Series power windows, in keeping with other imports and quite a few domestic specialty cars, were slow in operation. BMW introduced faster lifters for 1979. The air-conditioning in the 5 Series was also in keeping with contemporary imports by not being integrated. Whether it was the dealer installed unit, featuring a central plastic dash vent pod, or the factory system with a flat central vent grille, neither system could blend air conditioned air with heated air to create dry, warm air.

Around 6000-7000 US 528is were sold in the US in each of its three years of production. This took the grand total for US E12s to nearly 50,000 cars, slightly less than Corvette sales for a single year in the late seventies. It was not without teething problems, but, overall, things finished on the happy side of par. We all have to learn to walk before we can run!

A late '70s soft toy E12, made by San Diego company TfA (Toys for Adults) with artist Margie Smith. (Courtesy Ulrich Thieme)

3

E12 HIGH TECH – ECOLOGY, PERFORMANCE & SAFETY

BMW POWER TEAMS

For the United Kingdom and continental European markets the E12 5 Series was available in a myriad of forms. With BMW's growing sixties success the number of engine and gearbox permutations expanded. Thus, by the time the E12 came onto the scene in the early seventies, the possible variations were numerous. Being a middle child, the E12 could draw on options available to the 02/3 Series class and the higher echelon six-cylinder saloon, coupé/6/7 Series variants. Indeed, looking over the E12's run one can identify no less than three engine layouts, six different gearbox variations, twelve different power outputs – and a partridge in a pear tree!

To get things rolling initially we can look to the 1972 520 and 520i. Both were direct replacements for the earlier 2000 and 2000tii models. Whereas the 520i directly took over the Kugelfischer injected 2-litre M10, the 520 got a new twin carb spin.

In place of the previous single Solex downdraught carb was the first use by BMW of two Stromberg 175 CDET carbs, with automatic choke and central idle system for better starting, cold running and

synchronisation. This was just the opening stanza because BMW introduced the six-cylinder 525 at the 1973 Frankfurt Motor Show, and followed this with the larger engined 528 of 1974/5. The 525 and 528 represented the first time BMW had inserted the M30 big six into a mid range model.

Just as the Jaguar XJ6 was designed with the future V12 in mind, so too was the E12 5 Series designed to take BMW's M30. The E12's predecessor was exclusively motivated by the four pot M10, but the 5 Series was designed to accept both the M10 and M30. The 525/528 cars featured hardware upgrades over the M10-powered 520/520i to harness the new M30's power safely and reliably. There were four wheel discs, an upgraded cooling system, heavier duty front springs and the larger, sturdier manual gearboxes used on the contemporary six-cylinder saloons and coupés.

Testers felt the new six-cylinder E12s fell a bit short in terms of performance. *Motor* magazine praised the 525's ride, handling compromise and well laid out, comfortable interior, but felt the 2.5-litre motor didn't deliver the punch it expected. There was some feeling that the 525 didn't

The fuel crisis inspired development of the 1976 BMW 520 Wasserstoff, or Hydrogen5. (Courtesy Ulrich Thieme)

There is no rear deck filler flap, because Hydrogen5 runs on hydrogen alone. (Courtesy Ulrich Thieme)

The hydrogen tank takes up a lot of space. BMW's 2007 Hydrogen7 E65 760Li concealed the tank behind the rear seat.
(Courtesy Ulrich Thieme)

offer much ultimate performance advantage over the 520i. The larger engined version definitely lacked the 520i's eager feeling. These impressions were probably heightened by the fact that BMW had a number of more potent M30s in regular production by this stage.

With motors like the injected 3.2 and carb 3.3 M30s used in the 1974-77 3.3L/Li, it's understandable that some wondered why BMW didn't have more potent off-the-peg 5s. Part of the reason is that

To run on hydrogen, the 2-litre M10 used adapted fuel-injection, which had a Bosch L-jet AFM. This red E12 could indeed turn the planet green! (Courtesy Ulrich Thieme)

BMW also did Hydrogen7s based on the E23 and E38 7 Series saloons' units. However, mainstream motorists still rely on petroleum distillate. (Courtesy Ulrich Thieme)

Germany, and continental Europe in general, tends to have its road tax and insurance figures based on horsepower ratings and engine capacity. The 525/528 were set up to fall within the 150bhp and 170bhp fiscal cut-off points in West Germany. In addition, the cars had twin carb motors, Solex/Zenith 35/40 INATs, in a more laid-back form than that of the zesty 520i.

To compound matters, BMW gave the senior flagship 2500/2800 a 5bhp advantage to maintain the established model hierarchy, leaving the 525/528 on 145bhp and 165bhp respectively. However, the more expensive six-cylinder E12 525/528 were in a different class to the M10-powered 520/520i. They fitted the description of refined,

executive express very well; the sort of car to cover continental autoroutes at high continuous speeds for long periods with little strain on car or owner. In June 1974, *Thoroughbred & Classic Cars* mentioned, at a time when it still did features on new cars, that the 525 was a neat, efficient car and good value for money even at 4099 pounds sterling. The magazine felt there was little to criticise.

For 1977 BMW restyled the E12 to keep it in line with the corporate look shared by the 3, 6 and soon to arrive 7 Series. Gone was the E12's rectangular bonnet bulge, necessary to accommodate the long, flat, rectangular air filter box present on the 525/528. In its place was a narrow, bonnet-length

raised band with a tapered kidney grille, first seen on Paul Bracq's 1972 BMW Turbo. At the back the tail lamps were made larger with lens covers to match the new 7 Series cars. In addition, the fuel filler was repositioned to the side of the car.

The E12 dashboard also saw the arrival of moveable vent grilles. Several journals, including *Which?*, when testing a 520 in 1974, noted that the previous fixed grilles allowed air to be blown past the car's occupants. Very early 5 Series cars had the dash vent grilles painted in a contrasting light grey, but, by this time, they were a matching black. The '78 MY also saw the integration of the air-conditioning temperature and

According to factory figures – and BMW figures are known for being on the conservative side – the European specification 528i was good for 129mph. (Courtesy Ulrich Thieme)

BMW offered just one style of alloy rim in the 1970s. Up until 1974/5, the five-spoke Mahle rim sufficed; for the rest of the decade the Alpina turbine style pattern took over. This E12 has genuine 16-inch Alpina rims. (Courtesy Ulrich Thieme)

blower speed controls on factory air conditioned cars; previously, temperature and blower speed controls were separate. In addition, the stereo unit, if one was present, was no longer at the base of the console on air conditioned cars, but was now positioned higher.

On the engine front the 525/528 cars now had a single carb, and power outputs boosted to 150bhp and 170bhp respectively. Bigger changes were taking place lower in the range with the 2-litre cars. The 115bhp 520 and 125bhp 520i were both replaced by the new 122bhp 520/6, powered initially by a single Solex 4A1 version of the new M60 baby six, the final new engine released with Alex von Falkenhausen as head of engine design.

The new motor was intended to bring six-cylinder power and refinement to the 3 Series. BMW's Adolf Fischer was also on the design team of the M60, which took over from the M10 as BMW's mainstream representative in the 2-litre class. Its rubber cambelt played no small role in establishing the M60's great reputation for refinement. *Motor* was moved to say that the 2-litre six was the smoothest six in the world.

1978 saw the 528 replaced with the electronically injected 177bhp 528i. Earlier electronically injected bimmers, like the 3.0Si and 3.0 CSi, featured Bosch D-jetronic injection. D-jet, the world's first electronic fuel-injection, worked out the optimal air/fuel mix based on vacuum pressure of the intake manifold.

Using vacuum as the basis for the computer calculation, made the setup susceptible to false readings due to various unwanted motor vacuum leaks. The 528i, and US 530i, featured L-jetronic, which based its measurement on air aspirated through its airflow meter or AFM. The German word for air is luft, therefore, L-jetronic. L-jet and its mechanical brother K-jet, came out in 1973 as a technical second wave to 1968's D-jet.

With L-jet, a moveable air flap in the AFM would have its position relayed via a potentiometer to the engine management computer located in the glovebox. With D-jet the computer was so large it had to reside under the front passenger seat, where it would work out how long the injector solenoids should stay open. For '80 MY, the 528i models sold in some parts of continental Europe received the higher compression 184bhp motor shared with the 628CSi/728i. Compression ratio had also risen from 9.0 to 9.3:1.

The 528i was as large as one could go in continental Europe without encountering substantially higher road tax and insurance charges. For much of Europe, that's a limit of 2.8 litres and for Italy just 2 litres. Some may recall the shortlived 2.8-litre, XK-engined XJ6 created with an eye to such continental markets. Combine this with the two seventies gas crunches and generally high European prices for petroleum distillate, and it's readily apparent why the 2.8-litre 5 Series was the largest motored regular model for much of the time.

FUEL CRISIS WOES
In a period of economic slump, escalating fuel prices and spiralling inflation, BMW was weathering the storm rather well. In spite of decreasing economic activity and cost push inflation, BMW finished the first half of 1974 in the black. By the close of April it had managed to shift more US bimmers than in the whole of 1973. Sales were up in Britain and France, too. While the US big three, Volkswagen and Ford of West Germany were in dire straits, BMW was not doing too badly. Just in case you thought fat cat buyers were keeping BMW in the groove, remember that this was the time when higher echelon Anglo/Italian/US hybrids like the Iso, Jensen and Monteverdi, took a real commercial hammering. Even the wealthy were thinking twice before autographing their cheques!

America introduced its 55mph speed limit, Britain launched a temporary 50mph limit, and even the Bonn government of West Germany applied speed restrictions to what were usually unrestricted sections of the autobahn, which was so quiet it could be walked across without danger! BMW was getting on the belt-tightening wagon by introducing economy oriented, small-engined versions of existing ranges. The 1974 2500CS, 1502 and 90bhp 518 were all largely devoid of lavish trim. The 2500CS was commercially outgunned by its more powerful and expensive big brother, the 3.0CS.

In contrast, the 1502 and 518 were big hits in continental Europe. The 1502 saw out 02 production and the 518 became a regular fixture. As ever, the British market was less impressed by overtly value conscious BMWs. *Autocar* felt the 518 was sluggish and buyers would be wiser purchasing the swifter and more economical Ford Cortina 2000 or Vauxhall Cavalier 1900. Meanwhile, continental

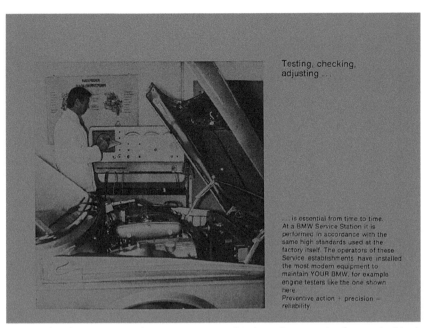

Testing, checking, adjusting . . .

. . . is essential from time to time. At a BMW Service Station it is performed in accordance with the same high standards used at the factory itself. The operators of these Service establishments have installed the most modern equipment to maintain YOUR BMW, for example engine testers like the one shown here.
Preventive action + precision = reliability.

Rationalised servicing and easier car ownership have been major factors behind the popularity of German cars for many years. (Courtesy BMW)

Europeans were miffed because an auto 518 wasn't available! As far as Britain was concerned *Autocar* mentioned, in mid 1979, that the 520i was the most popular E12 variant. In Europe, sales of the 520i were limited because buyers felt it offered little extra performance compared to the 520, in light of its much higher price.

Through the tough times BMW stuck to its credo of high quality cars that needed little looking after. 1971/72 saw the introduction of the fusebox-mounted computer diagnosis connector. Sensors in

By now tuner Hartge had been going for ten years. The firm was transitioning from the 10:1 CR 220bhp Hartge 535i E12, to the new E28 5 Series. (Courtesy Hartge)

Between November 1981 and May 1982, Alpina made the B7S. At over 160mph, with 0-60mph in under 6 seconds, it was the world's fastest *four-door* car! (Courtesy Ulrich Thieme)

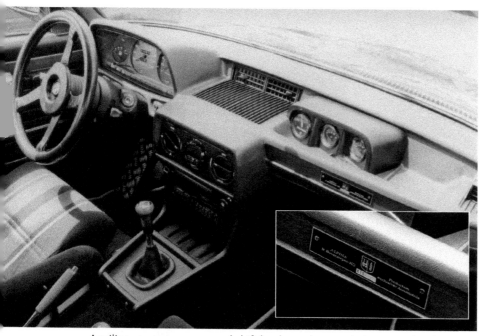

Auxiliary gauges, rosewood shift knob, and transmission tunnel turbo boost adjuster (up to 12.5psi) all spelt *high-performance* business. (Courtesy Ulrich Thieme)

Dolomite in 1973. Originating in the sixties, the Triumph saloon's development slowed during the British Leyland era. The decision that Triumph should focus on sports cars didn't help the Dolomite, either. However, *Which?* had to concede that it was a comfortable, practical and swift model which was popular with readers. Even so, the magazine couldn't recommend ownership of the car beyond its comprehensive one year British Leyland 'Supercover' warranty period. Remedying the numerous faults which cropped up outside of warranty could be pricey. This reliability problem didn't affect the BMW 520 *Which?* tested in 1974. The report simply stated "... if finding 3500 pounds sterling is a simple matter for you, and you buy the 520 in the hope of finding it a fast, comfortable and reliable car, then you'll probably think your money well spent".

BMW had a very low public profile in Britain at the start of the seventies; by the decade's end the company was practically as well known as the Goodies! The import and sale of BMWs was handled by BMW Concessionaires GB Pty Ltd, a subsidiary of the Cooper Group. The company was based at Portslade near Brighton, and checked, repaired and distributed cars to the various dealers.

As Alan Pavey told *Practical Classics* years later, in those days the dealers didn't have to do anything! BMW Concessionaires even did right-hand drive

the car relayed input to the Sun diagnosis computer sitting in the BMW dealership, resulting in readouts on carb tune, distributor dwell angle or flywheel alignment being available from oscillographs in 6 to 8 minutes. Reliability at a time when mass market cars proffered less than consumers expected was definitely of some worth.

Which? said as much when testing popular British Leyland group member the Triumph

To combat turbo lag, Alpina upped the B7's displacement from 3.0 to 3.5 litres. The B7 and B7S were also available for the E24 6 series. (Courtesy Ulrich Thieme)

conversions on the 2800 CS, and a one-off conversion for Stirling Moss on a 2000tii hatchback with custom quadraphonic stereo, although by the time the E12 came along, BMW was in the habit of creating factory right-hand drive versions for just about all its models.

During the seventies the strategy was low volume and high prices. By the late seventies British buyers that formerly used to purchase Rovers, Triumphs, Wolseleys and Jaguars were increasingly choosing Saabs, Volvos, Audis and BMWs. Buyers developed a taste for cars with a background of good build quality and thorough development. It had become common in Britain's car industry for a model to be hastily released. A revised Mk II version, with faults that should have been eliminated pre-launch, would come subsequently. After that the model was left to fend for itself in the face of younger, developed opposition.

In 1980, BMW took over the import and sale of its cars in Britain, just as it had done five years earlier in North America.

Autocar described the steady path that allowed BMW, and other continental car makers, to win over British buyers as the years progressed. When testing the BMW 316 in January 1982, the magazine concluded: "Owners will appreciate many of the features, particularly the responsiveness and good engineering, that have contributed to BMW's steady success, even in this relatively low cost example." After taking over from BMW Concessionaires, BMW decided that, as it already had a foot in the door, now was the time to price more competitively and go for greater volume.

In 1981 sales in Britain leapt to 17,086 units, and by early November 1982 passed 20,000 units for the first time. BMW GB boss, Dr Walter Hasselkus, remarked at the time how amazed he was at their ability to sell an ever increasing number of BMWs in Britain.

By now well into the eighties, and Margaret Thatcher's Britain of yuppies and filofaxes, BMW's reputation was as assured as its used car warranty! The storm clouds of economic depression were lifting, everyone around the globe wanted a fancy set of wheels, and had the money to get them.

Ten years earlier it hadn't been so easy to sell high profile performance cars. Heightened worldwide interest in fuel prices and the environment put the kibosh on symbols of perceived excess consumption. The new Daimler-Benz W116 S class saloon, replete with V8 petrol engine, didn't get a warm reception from all at the 1973 Geneva Motor Show. Similarly, the West German public and press gave the 1973 2002 Turbo, Europe's first turbo car, the cold shoulder. It precipitated removal of the '2002 Turbo' mirror script from the front spoiler and contributed to its premature death.

As in the US, the West German government announced in the early seventies that leaded petrol would be gradually phased out. The 1972 520/520i had engines designed to accept fuel with a limit of 0.4gm/litre lead content. BMW's M10 and M30 had redesigned combustion chambers, with altered squish areas, to allow the use of lower octane fuel without drastic reductions in engine compression and efficiency. The European Common Market was moving along similar environmental lines.

Back in the mid '60s, the 1500 – the 5 Series' predecessor – marked Alpina's first association with the BMW marque when a special dual carb kit was created. The E12 5 Series saw Alpina's transition from tuner to car maker: the B7 and B7S are fitting reminders of this change. (Courtesy Michel Darbellay)

When you have a blown M30 producing 330 horses with maximum boost at 12.5psi, it's necessary to deviate from stock in some areas. The bottom end was fine; BMW's tests of M1 turbos showed the M30 could cope with almost double normal bmep levels without major modification. However, sodium filled valves and special intake/exhaust manifolds were used. The changes were critical on the exhaust side, given the high temperature of exhaust gases associated with turbo motors. (Courtesy Michel Darbellay)

1975 was the final year BMW used Kugelfischer mechanical and Bosch D-jetronic electronic injection on its cars, replaced by Bosch K-jetronic and Bosch L-jetronic respectively for 1976.

Emissions control was also a big reason BMW replaced the Solex/Zenith carbs with the single four barrel Solex 4A1, and even that gave way to Bosch L-jet in Europe by 1978. If you think this was tough, you don't know North America. Pollution laws were tighter at an earlier date and required more elaborate measures, culminating in the system used on the 1979 US 528i, which is pretty similar to the emissions system used on the majority of cars driven today. BMW designed the M30, used in the 1968/9 2500/2800, to cope with America's first wave of 1968

With a trucklike 332 pounds per foot of torque, the Alpina B7S resulted in ZF making a custom manual gearbox called ZF S5-40. All units/parts have been sold to Alpina or the Tom Walkinshaw Racing team, so if you want a rebuild for your hot E12, don't go to ZF, the cupboards are bare! (Courtesy Michel Darbellay)

Alpina's body graphics still figure on its latest models; some form of contemporary folk art, perhaps? (Courtesy Ulrich Thieme)

certified with the Environmental Protection Authority, so BMW kept US six-cylinder choices down to a 3-litre manual or auto. Each all-new package would have to run on the EPA's chassis dyno for 50,000 miles, with emissions testing at 4000 mile intervals.

Things got heavy in 1973 and 1975. 1973 saw nitrogen oxides being monitored for the first time in emission testing: up until that point hydrocarbons and carbon monoxide had been the sole areas. The trouble was that two-way catalytic converters used by most car makers had little effect on nitrogen oxides. To make matters worse, 1975 saw emissions regulations grip tighter still. From here on in just about all cars sold in the US had to resort to catalytic converters to pass Californian emissions regulations. In the other 49 states there was still room to manoeuvre, at least for the present.

BMW's big six had been getting away with murder up to 1975. Apart from the compression drop for 1972 and expected adjustment to fuel mixture and ignition timing, it was business as usual. The triple hemi head meant it had avoided exhaust gas recirculation (EGR) or air pumps. 1975 would be different and the only 3-litre offered, in the 530i and 3.0Si, had quite a few changes: Bosch L-jet fuel-injection, EGR, twin thermal reactors and an air pump. EGR directed exhaust gases back into the intake ports. The air pump injected air into the exhaust ports to make the fuel mixture leaner. The twin thermal reactors were chambers on the exhaust manifold dealing with the motor's waste produce.

The whole idea was to get a more thorough burn inside and

pollution laws without any add-on devices.

The triple hemi cylinder head, with spheres around the sparkplug, intake and exhaust valves, burnt the fuel/air mix so thoroughly that the only deviation from European versions was lean carb settings. That was okay for the late sixties, but the laws got stricter. At first, larger engines were allowed to emit more pollutants, but eventually the

test entailed an absolute level for all engines. The phasing out of lead in fuel brought an across-the-board lowering of compression ratios. 1971 was the last year for the nine to one compression, 99 octane premium fed twin carb US 2.8-litre M30. From 1972, BMW offered a low compression 3-litre that ran on 91 octane leaded regular.

It cost a great deal to get each drivetrain package emissions

The BMW M30 I6 had a triple hemi cylinder head to fight pollution. The Kugelfischer injected M10 I4 is shown at the bottom. (Courtesy BMW)

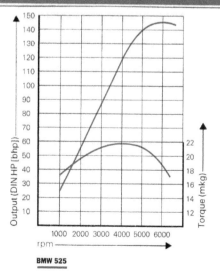

BMW 525

Back in 1974, H&B was a West Coast Alpina agent called Alpina/West. Here, its 530i is being pushed hard at Sears Point. (Courtesy H&B)

outside the combustion chamber so that as many nasties as possible were eliminated before exiting the tailpipe. Bosch L-jet came along to ensure that in the midst of the emission's party the car was still able to start, restart and run reasonably smoothly. The 1975 530i made 176bhp net, compared to 165bhp net for the base motored 1975 Corvette. Contemporary road tests put a stick shift 530i midway between the base 350 Vette and the 1975 L82-engined version for 0 to 60 sprinting.

The 1976 US Mercedes 280S was 40bhp down on the European version. When the Lancia Beta Monte Carlo made the trip Stateside in the guise of the desmogged Lancia Scorpion, even the normally conservative *R&T* was moved to call it a eunuch. However, the 1975 US 530i was 11 ponies up on the top dog in Europe, the 165bhp 528! The laws didn't stick there, but got even stricter. By 1979 both BMW and Honda couldn't continue with their alternative emissions theory.

With Honda it was the stratified engine, segmenting the combustion chamber into an area of lean fuel mixture and a smaller area of rich fuel mix. By using a three valve cylinder head the end result complied with pollution regulations without a catalytic converter.

For BMW it was the thermal reactor approach. By 1979/80 neither could ignore the catalytic converter any more. In 1976 Saab and then Volvo used the three-way catalytic converter and Bosch lambda sond exhaust mounted oxygen sensor. It could keep an eye on hydrocarbons, carbon monoxide and nitrogen oxide. The oxygen sensor fed a corrective signal to the engine management computer to keep the fuel mixture at the stoichiometric ratio.

BMW was able to dump the

With Alpina parts not so suited to US conditions, the alternative was the 1980 H&B 528i. Now 100 per cent H&B, its 528i was the first US tuner-offered turnkey BMW. (Courtesy H&B)

EGR, air pump and twin thermal reactors. The 1979 US 528i got by in a single 50 state version, a first for a US 5, using just the three-way cat and a diet of 91 octane unleaded. The changeover killed several birds with one stone. A finite supply of leaded regular made the 530i an automotive stopgap. BMW's previous approach to emissions called for retarded ignition timing and a rich fuel mixture for the thermal reactors to do a thorough burn. Yes, the owner could take advantage of cheaper leaded regular but that wasn't going to last forever.

The ability to run more advanced ignition timing greatly improved the US 5 Series' engine response throughout the rev range when compared to the thermal reactor-equipped cars. Having two red hot thermal reactors, which could be seen to glow red at night, next

H&B was famous for its CK53 chassis set of three-piece modular rims, based on a BBS design, with an H&B centre, and more rounded spokes than Alpina's 16-inch hoops. (Courtesy H&B)

As with other US firms, H&B had bolt on turbo kits for M10s & M30s. With the six that implied 250 net horses ... giddyup!! (Courtesy H&B)

to the delicate aluminium cylinder head wasn't a good thing either. A propensity for head cracking precipitated a lawsuit against BMW, culminating in BMW North America offering replacement heads to affected owners even if the car was out of warranty. The head was redesigned with bigger water jackets for 1980, but getting rid of the twin nuclear reactors was extra insurance!

So the US 528i could have more advanced timing and a leaner fuel mixture than the 530i, that meant better economy. Why would an EPA window gas mileage sticker suddenly be of such great import? The reason was CAFE, or Corporate Average Fleet Economy. Late in 1975 Congress passed the Energy Policy and Conservation Act. Federal legislation that forced cars sold in North America to become more frugal. Cars sold in the US would have to meet a fleet average, starting with 18mpg in 1978 and

progressively rising to 27.5mpg by 1985, or the car company selling in the US would face a gas guzzler tax on versions that couldn't meet the average.

In 1978 *Consumer Union* said it feared that BMW and Rolls-Royce would have to leave the US because they had no hope of meeting CAFE. Well, RR just faced up to the tax and soldiered on. BMW dumped its leaded, thermal reactor approach and was in the clear for the eighties. Replacing the 528i's, and other US bimmers', standard four-speed with an overdrive five-speed for 1980 also helped. All's well that ends well, I guess!

Self-preservation ranked right up there with protecting the environment and preserving fuel resources. Safety and the consumer rights movement made the '70s the era of the ESV rather than the SUV! The US National Highway Traffic and Safety Administration initiated the Experimental Safety Vehicle

project. Prototypes were built and submitted under contract to the US government from GM, AMF, the Fairchild Corporation and others, to show the level of safety which could be built into everyday cars.

Daimler Benz, with the ESF 13, Volvo and BMW with their 1972 gullwing Turbo were all playing it safe. The BMW experimental vehicle featured a deformable nose section, rigid survival cell, padded interior and grouped controls. By the mid seventies, the spectre of overloaded tyres, hostile exterior and interior projections, a lack of seatbelts and poorly positioned gas tanks had been overcome, at least in a legislative sense.

Federal Safety Standard FSS 215, effective from January 1 1972, made front outboard three-point belts with a warning light and buzzer mandatory. For 1973, cars sold in the US had to withstand a 5mph front and 2.5mph rear end impact without damage to safety

Alpina/West became Hardy & Beck, then H&B as Allen Hardy alone ran the company, Hans Beck having parted. Today, H&B offers all the spoilers, chassis and stripes to recreate its '80s funmobiles. (Courtesy H&B)

related hardware. FSS 208 saw the introduction of 'interlock,' a mini logic sequence computer that wouldn't let the 1974 US market car start unless the driver closed the door, buckled up and activated the ignition, in that order. The use of inertia reel retractors for the shoulder portion of the front three-point belts was also planned. On the 530i's dash rail was a warning pod with lights for EGR, thermal reactor inspection and seatbelt usage.

The bumper basher test was upgraded with a car being subjected to repeated blows from a

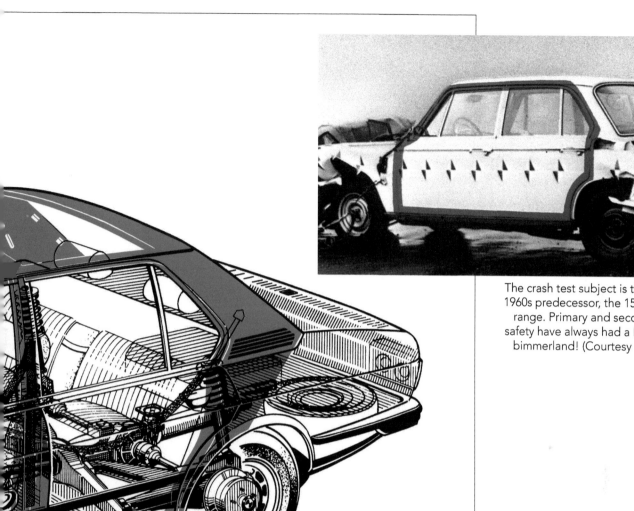

The crash test subject is the E12's 1960s predecessor, the 1500-2000 range. Primary and secondary safety have always had a home in bimmerland! (Courtesy BMW)

The red lines denote the E12's rigid passenger safety cell, the part of the car intended to stay intact after the front and rear crumple zones have absorbed the energy of an impact. (Courtesy BMW)

Fear of proposed mandatory roll-over tests resulted in targa tops being the main choice for fresh air motoring for a number of years. (Courtesy BMW)

narrow, pendulum-shaped object, and the rear impact test stepped up to 5mph. The pendulum strike point could be anywhere between 16 and 20 inches from the ground, making standardised ride heights essential for US sold cars. US insurance companies didn't like shelling out dough to repair damaged radiators and air-conditioning condensers so they pushed the US government to bring on the 5mph impact requirements. As *Consumer Union* noted, these laws were to protect the car, not the occupants!

Interlock was given the heave-ho post-1974. Automakers had agreed with the US government that they wouldn't make a dime of profit from safety-related equipment. As far as the manufacturers were concerned, life-saving interlock was just so much automotive ballast, and they were able to use their muscle to consign it to history after just one year.

The E12 was designed with safety very much in mind. Possessing a more rigid unibody

Note the black plaque recording a 1972 'USA' E3 roof strength test. BMW withdrew its pillarless CS coupés from the US at the end of 1974. (Courtesy BMW)

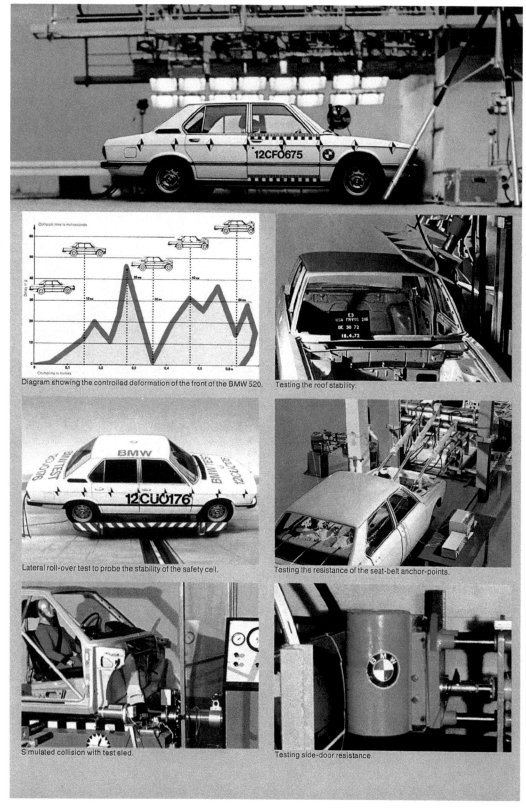

Diagram showing the controlled deformation of the front of the BMW 520.

Testing the roof stability.

Lateral roll-over test to probe the stability of the safety cell.

Testing the resistance of the seat-belt anchor-points.

Simulated collision with test sled.

Testing side-door resistance.

than that of its predecessor, front and rear crumple zones, collapsible steering column and dished steering wheel with padded boss, were all features. The mandatory US reinforced side bars were also in evidence. A concealed roof bar lay at the centre of the E12's centre section as insurance against roll over, quashing plans for a convertible. BMW stopped selling the pillarless CS coupé in America at the end of 1974. Its replacement, the 6 series, had a built-in roll bar concealed by painting the central pillar black. Finally, Jaguar's XKE

replacement, the XJS, would have to wait many years before a real ragtop was offered.

The US 530i complied with all US dictates. Its 5mph bumpers were rubber-clad aluminium bars mounted on hydraulic rams, with the gap between the extended bumpers and carbody filled with rubber and capped with concertina corner concealers. Many were relieved that BMW didn't standardise these 'rubber baby buggy bumpers' for all world markets like Volvo and Porsche!

Lighting was another area to

contend with. The US legislative dislike of unequal sized lamps and rectangular reflectors meant that 2000 and 2000CS BMWs going Stateside had to ditch their trapezoidal eyewear in favour of pairs of equal sized round lamps in a trapezoidal frame. This was probably a contributing factor to BMW using four same sized headlamps from that point on. The 530i also had side marker lamps, orange at the front and red at the rear. They were familiar on US market cars from 1969 onwards and lit the car up like a Christmas tree!

BMW's 1972 Turbo Gullwing, mid engined safety showcar, led the athletes' parade at the 1972 Munich Olympics. The BMW E12 5 series, was revealed a few days after the games. (Courtesy BMW)

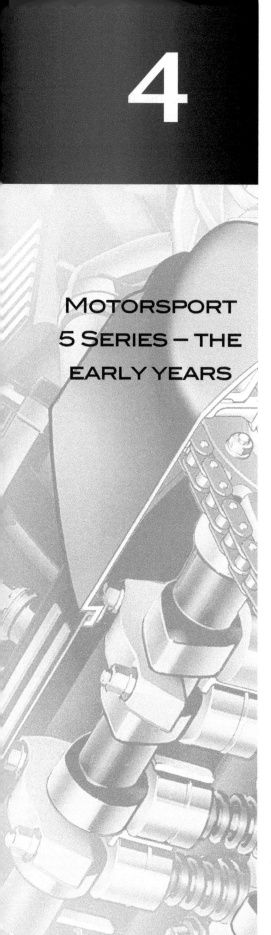

4

MOTORSPORT 5 SERIES – THE EARLY YEARS

Motorsport boss Jochen Neerpasch and crew turned E12s into hotrods on request! (Courtesy BMW)

The legendary Bob Lutz was briefly BMW's marketing man, and pushed for the creation of BMW Motorsport GmbH in 1972. Motorsport oversaw BMW's racing activities, but its first boss, Jochen Neerpasch, quickly developed a lucrative sideline. Motorsport division made special E12 5 Series cars for wealthy patrons, and part contributing racers like Ronnie Peterson and Gunnar Nilsson.

Adding larger 3.0/3.3 I6s from the E3 and E9, as well as vented

The E12 M535i was good for 0-60mph in 7 seconds, and 140mph, and was faster and torquier than the 3.0CSL Batmobile. (Courtesy Andreas Gattingers)

Nigel Mansell bought a new white 1980 E12 M535i. This is a gray market example.
(Courtesy Adam Wilson)

disc brakes, lsd etc from BMW's parts shelf proved popular and wise. After the fuel crisis, many racing departments were either scaled back or closed. Ex racer and owner of BMW Concessionaires UK, Jonathan Sieff, had a special 1974 530 built by Motorsport using engine and hardware from the 3.0CSL.

For '77 MY, Motorsport offered a formal catalogue model with the 533i. It resembled a normal series two E12 528, with lattice 14 x 7in alloys. However, the rear boot lid badging said 533i on its black plaque. Fitted with an injected 3205cc M30 making 200bhp, factory figures were 0-100kmph in 7.9 seconds, and 210kmph top speed. Price started from 29,500 DM. You could leave the car plain, have no exterior badging, or add options as before. Wealthy West German

In 50-70mph acceleration using the lowest gear possible (3rd), *Autocar* found the E12 M535i, E28 M5 and E34 M5 3.6 all took 3.9 seconds. (Courtesy Stuart Brown)

BMW Motorsport has stated that the E12 M535i was the development basis for the E28 M5. Motorsport had tested the 24-valve M88 in the E12 M535i.

An E12 M535i being pursued by an AC Schnitzer E36 3 Series at Castle Combe. (Courtesy Stuart Brown)

The E12 M535i's standard Getrag 265 CR five-speed, Scheel buckets and optional a/c are present.
(Courtesy Julien Gaudy)

patrons liked sleepers to keep tree huggers and socialists at bay.

Up to the 533i, Motorsport hand-built its special 5 Series from scratch. Now, it hand-finished base cars from Dingolfing. In 1980-81 a new model ... the M535i! It was a curtain raiser to the new E28 5 Series. The M535i came with M90 I6 and a varying specification. 1410 cars were built, including 450 RHD UK cars. Britain was going to get 200 M535is, but the model proved most popular. UK spec involved front and rear 530MLE spoilers, sports suspension with Bilsteins, 3.07 lsd, 14 x 6.5 in Mahle lattice alloys, CR dogleg five-speed, Recaro buckets in black cloth or

leather, E23 7 series front discs, and E26 M1 tiller.

Not all M535is had the bodykit, but all had an engine oil cooler behind the front valence, just like M90-powered 1978-82 635CSis and 735is. The M90 was a M88, with higher 9.3:1 CR and M30 head. *Autocar*'s figures for 0-60 mph, top speed and economy for the respective M535i and 3.0CSL were 7.1 seconds/139mph/20.2mpg versus 7.3 seconds/133mph/16.7mpg. The same journal's Jag XKE V12 4 speed's figures were 7.2 seconds/143 mph/15mpg.

Reasons for not using the M1's engine? Motorsport was busy

making 400 M88s so the M1 could get homologated. For another, the M88 was dry sump only, and had an expensive and unique Kugelfischer-Bosch injection system, plus electronic flywheel-triggered ignition. However, in road-going form the early M88 wasn't fully honed. Its job was to get the M1 homologated quickly, and only had a 9.0:1 CR, 277bhp at 6500rpm and 239lb/ft at 5000rpm. The M90 made 218bhp at 5200rpm and 229lb/ft at 4000rpm. In practice, an E12 M5 with M88 would have been only 0.5 seconds quicker to sixty, and 5mph faster on top speed, but less torquey and a lot pricier. M90 torque tore the

895 Motorsport 5 Series pre-dated the E12 M535i. The M90 tested the viability of the M88's siamesed bores.
(Courtesy Julien Gaudy)

M535i side loader lsd from its boot floor mounting! A factory fix kit was devised.

THE FIRST M CAR – 530MLE

BMW SA's 530 Motorsport Limited Edition was an homologation special that looked just like the later E12 M535i, but powered by a tuned version of the twin carb engine used in the BMW 3.0S. It featured drilled aluminium dress panels to save weight, and even had its battery mounted in a cut-out in the boot for better weight distribution.

The 201 road cars sold allowed BMW Suid Afrik to compete in local touring car racing. Development of the racing 530MLEs was overseen by Jochen Neerpasch and assistant

The South African 530MLE, a homologation special that allowed BMW Suid Afrik to field a two car team in local touring car races. (Courtesy Klaus Wiehl)

The 201 530MLE road cars represented the first time that BMW formally offered a Motorsport model for sale to the general public.

Drilled aluminium dress panels make the 530MLE stand out among Motorsport cars. A boot floor cut-out was utilised for the battery in the interest of more even weight distribution. (Both courtesy Klaus Wiehl)

Eddie Keizan, with team mates Alain Lavoipierre/Paddy Driver, dominated South African saloon racing. The cars lapped Kyalami in 1min 36s at 220kph, versus 1min 17s at 260kph for Formula 1 cars. (Courtesy Ulrich Thieme)

Martin Braungart, the two Ford of West Germany escapees who sprinkled fairy dust over the factory CS coupés to bestow success in the European Touring Car Championship.

Between 1976 and mid 1978, the terrible two 530MLEs cleaned up on the track, with 15 straight victories at one stage. One racing car was built at the Motorsport factory in West Germany, the other racer and road versions were put together in South Africa. The racing 530MLE was jointly developed by BMW Motorsport and AC Schnitzer. The former even flew the development car to the latter, using Sabena Airlines!

In South African metric speak, the racing motor made 202kW at 6750 rpm and 318Nm at 5500rpm. The 530MLE racer could hit 235kph in fifth. Bilstein dampers and Dunlop tires wrapped around Chaparral rims were the rolling stock, 406mm tall, 279mm wide at the front and 305mm wide at the rear. Tyres front and rear were 275/600mm and 300/625mm respectively, all housed by flared arches.

The 530MLE debut was at the Republic Day Trophy race, held on June 5 1976. Also in 1976, the BMW CSL returned to the ETCC after a year in US IMSA racing.

The road cars had 147kW, but the 3x2bbl Solex 40/36 racing 3 litres had the touch of BMW's Paul Rosche ('Camshaft Paul'), and 202kW! (Courtesy Ulrich Thieme)

With Motorsport stripes and sponsorship from BIC, Salora TV and Castrol, the racing 530MLEs looked as good as they moved. However, by 1978 the Mazda Rotary Capella (RX2) coupés had brought stiff opposition.
(Courtesy Ulrich Thieme)

The chrome side mirrors suggest a 1979 BMW M533i. (Courtesy BMW)

5

THE EVOLUTIONARY E28 5 SERIES

BMW's return to success seemed straightforward. The Quandt family exerted its influence greatly, following the failed Daimler-Benz takeover. Quandt family selected management, and financial aid from a small West German bank, allowed the game changing New Class BMW 1500-2000 to find its feet.

Between 1963 and 1970, BMW turnover accelerated at never less than 14% per annum. The entire period was profitable. On the eve of the new E12 5 Series, a young 42-year-old managing director called Eberhard von Kuenheim was appointed (*Management Today* January 1971, p49). The E12 5 Series continued BMW's good fortune, with around 738,000 produced. It would be a hard act to follow.

However, BMW had an answer for the '80s in the form of the E28 chassis 5 Series of 1981/2. *Motor*'s Martin Hodder wrote about the smugness and confidence exuded

An E28 520i is shown. With the initial E28, only the humble 518 lacked injection. However, for 1985 the 90bhp 518 was replaced with the 105 horse 518i.

(Courtesy Stephan Becker)

The popular 520i's baby six, was upgraded from 125 to 129bhp for 1986. The smoothest engine this side of a Jag V12, but lacking low end torque. (Courtesy Stephan Becker)

The clean, functional styling of Claus Luthe featured less chrome than the previous 5 Series.
(Courtesy Billy Isbell)

by BMW's PR characters during the model's first announcement before the world press, in spite of the absence of an initial 3.5-litre variant.

It would be fair to say that BMW's answer wasn't the one the press was expecting. The hot topic of debate was how similar in appearance the new E28 was to its E12 predecessor. BMW's Claus Luthe, formerly at Audi, was in charge of styling and, in a subsequent interview, mentioned that he was given a specific directive to go conservative. It is a fact that the E28 was the most conservative out of three styling proposals presented.

THE INVISIBLE MAKEOVER
It could be said that never before has a new model looked so similar, and yet, in substance, been so very different. The situation was succinctly explained by former chairman Eberhard von Kuenheim, when interviewed by Paul Frere. "For years the press has been complaining that the industry must be mad to invest so much money in mere cosmetic changes, rather than technical progress. Here, we spent money on a lot of technical improvements and you say we should have spent more on cosmetics!"

The Konigsberg-born head honcho was speaking the truth. The E28 was a completely re-engineered solution to the problems of the early eighties. Indeed, only the centre section of the E12 was carried over, all exterior panels were completely new and even half-an-inch was missing from the wheelbase this time around! In addition to the customary task of updating the

5 Series to incorporate general technical advances since the E12's 1972 launch, there was a specific requirement to adapt to the particular needs of fuel economy and environmental concerns.

While the E28 may not look greatly different to the outgoing E12, the new car's styling did receive a great deal of attention. In fact, never has a redesign been closer to the maxim that form must follow function. Alterations to the 5's profile were largely motivated by the need to improve its aerodynamic qualities. In the wake of world gas shortages, car makers had become keenly aware of the tremendous contribution good aerodynamics can make to substantial fuel economy improvements. In 1980 BMW started to use its first in-house wind tunnel testing facility, a move that would help the E28 reach its goals.

There was a need to reduce the 5's frontal area and generate greater downforce at the back. To this end the bonnet was resculpted for a quicker drop-off and smoother leading edge. The front spoiler area was redesigned to reduce lift, and the rear boot line was both raised and flattened to generate the extra downforce that was required. While the traditional BMW visage of circular lamps, kidney and reverse slope grille was retained, everything was made a touch shorter. Indeed, *R&T* was correct in stating that this would be the final new bimmer to feature the reverse slope front that had become part of the corporate furniture since the 1500 came on the scene.

Reshaping the profile wasn't the only way to make a car cleave through the air more easily. In

keeping with the work BMW did on the E12 in its twilight years, the E28 was put on a major diet to shed excess pounds. The obvious evidence of this was the decision to turf the forward opening, counterbalanced bonnet. Sure, it looked classy, and its ability to stay open without visible help was neat, but all this class weighed more than a conventional system. So the E28 changed to a rearward opening bonnet supported by gas struts.

Continuing on the subject of weight loss, the E28 utilised thinner glass and reduced sound padding to achieve targeted efficiency gains. Even thinner gauge steel was used for areas not critical to structural strength. The E28's bonnet is noticeably thinner and more prone to flexing when the owner waxes the car. The press kit accompanying the E28 outlined the breakdown of where the weight – or the money – went! All-up, some 90 to 100 kilos were eliminated from the weight of the average 5 Series variant.

The rear suspension semi trailing arms were made hollow by seam welding pressed shells together. Five-and-a-half kilos were pared by using a thinner, but more liberally ribbed, casting for the crankcase on the 528i. To balance the possible loss in refinement caused by removal of excess weight, more compliant engine mounts and a third muffler minimised any problems on the dba front. Paul Frere, in his Letter from Europe for *R&T*, mentioned how quiet the new E28 was at high speeds.

You can't go very far in discussing a company whose middle name is motor without talking engines. In this area the E28 offered more

73

An E28 wheel well accessory jerry can. With the new aero Audi 100 waiting in the wings, BMW was trying to make the E28 as frugal as possible. (Courtesy Derin Oloyede)

of the same with a weather eye out to achieve incremental gains in economy, performance and refinement. The three engine family consisting of the M10 small fours, M60 small sixes and M30 big sixes, were carried over with carefully considered modifications. With an engine range that other car makers – including Daimler-Benz – envy, it was wise to leave items that worked well alone.

Starting at the end of the sixties with the 2000tii, BMW's first fuel injected car, BMW initiated a pattern of having one fuel injected manual variant topper for each range. In the eighties BMW took this one step further by making fuel-injection universal for every variant. With the E28, only the 518 of 1981 to 1984 vintage featured a carb; all other versions made use of fuel-injection.

THE ARRIVAL OF BOSCH DME

The 520i used mechanical K-jetronic whilst the upmarket 525i and 528i used the more sophisticated L-jetronic. Both systems saw the light of day back in 1973. The K-jet version was a continuous high pressure setup and the L-jet version used a computer and based its decisions on airflow. The real news for the eighties 5 Series lay in the form of Bosch Digital Motor Electronics, first seen in the US on the 1982 528e: for a European 5 Series look to the similar 1983 525e. This DME system combined the hotwire air density sensor of Bosch LH with the incorporation of ignition timing into the engine management computer's sphere of influence.

The first time the engine management computer coped with fuel, air and ignition timing was ten years after the first fuel injected production BMW. The 1980 732i, part of the revised E23 range, was the acid test for this next step in improving economy, driveability and performance. It made sense to test out the new system on a single version of the low volume 7 Series.

No less than sixteen advance angles were programmed into the car's computer. Engine revolution was the independent variable, and another sixteen angles were available for changes in intake manifold pressure. This implied 256 choices for ignition timing.

In the 1980s, BMW quickly earned a reputation for being at the cutting edge of electronics. Even though major magazines considered Munich's boxy styling to be out of date, public brand perception was the opposite. BMW South Africa even had a funny TV ad. It introduced the new 1982 E12/8 5 Series, where the poor 'ol carb was given an actual funeral! All new E12/8s had injection, you see.

While the US 528e and European 525e were being prepared, yesterday's solutions would have to suffice. K-jet, L-jet and the interim KE and LH would be the technical stepping stones allowing the E28 and other cars to deal with immediate concerns. The initial range also witnessed marginal increases in engine compression to eke out the last drop of efficiency from high octane European fuel. 1981/1982 power outputs ranged from the 90bhp 518 and 125bhp 520i to the 150bhp 525i and 184bhp 528i. Class-leading power outputs which, when combined with the already mentioned weight reductions, placed the respective versions at the head of their various fields.

At the top end of town in Europe was the 528i, and, according to Britain's *Motor* magazine, it managed to out-accelerate the Audi 200 Turbo, and have a 5mph top speed buffer over the larger-engined V8 Rover 3500. With a

With E28 styling mostly constant, a personalised licence plate would have kept UK neighbours guessing the exact age of this 1987 528i. Britain has a letter/year plate index system. (Courtesy Jamie Myles)

Originally coming with TRX rims and overdrive five-speed, this 528i now has Alpina 16-inchers and close ratio five-speeder. (Courtesy Jamie Myles)

The interior of an Australian specification 1984 520i; from 1982 to 1985, only the 520i and 528i were available in this market. Note the standard factory air-conditioning activated by depressing the rectangular button bearing a snowflake symbol. The portion of the dash housing stereo, heating and air con controls was unique to air conditioned E28s.
(Author photo)

top speed of 130mph and a 0 to 60 time of under 8 seconds, plus excellent fuel consumption, it had the competition under heavy pressure. For its comparison *Motor* chose models as diverse as the Daimler-Benz 280E, Ford Granada 2.8 inj and the Talbot Tagora. The E28 was a commercial and critical success; its first year of sales in Britain saw a 70% increase over the E12's final year figures for the same market.

Superb power, refinement and economy were hardly surprising characteristics for a German company with a strong engineering basis, but what about handling? A US advert for the 2500/2800 range from the late sixties stated that BMW suspension was known for being even faster than BMW motors. While it may be too harsh to say that no truth stands forever, we could say that such truths become qualified.

As the sixties and seventies progressed, European cars – particularly export focused marques – were on a trend towards larger and more powerful motors. For example, with the dawn of the seventies, Daimler-Benz launched modern V8s of moderate displacement for its mainstream large models that were formerly exclusively six-cylinder cars.

Apart from the MB 250/280S, BMW had a few examples of

Bosch Motronic saw the distributor get junked as the ECU took over fuel mix and timing duties. Fewer mechanical items subject to wear promised a more reliable future. (Courtesy Bruce & Donna McDonald)

growth. The E12 5 Series was available with the company's big six, whereas its predecessor was a four pot model. It wouldn't be unfair to say that ultimate range models like the 1973/74 2002 Turbo and 1980/81 M535i required a careful hand if their excellent engines were to be exploited to the full. The former car had the slightly anti-social habit of being able to swap ends in a high speed bend if you concentrated hard enough in the dry, and with marginally less effort in the wet! Excellent cars, but they did require some input from the driver.

When Alex von Falkenhausen was asked about the 2002 Turbo's chosen power level of 170bhp, he did mention that a key reason was the ability and skill of potential purchasers. Given that anyone with a regular driving licence could buy the car, it would have been irresponsible to set up the engine to produce more power. BMW did the right thing by the average consumer and kept the power down to 170bhp.

Semi trailing arm rear suspension made its debut on the baby BMW 600, offering the advantages of swing arm and trailing arm. The setup became part of the engineering furniture at BMW in the ensuing years.

By the end of the seventies the 5 Series had a power spread ranging from 90bhp to 218bhp net. An uncommonly large spread for a European car. Within such an extensive model range one could see the point where the BMW chassis could become a handful. The 150bhp 525, and higher versions, could catch the inattentive offguard in certain situations, as it called for a level of concentration that was probably too much to ask from the average driver. BMW was possibly a victim of its own success in two ways. Firstly, BMWs were becoming increasingly popular and, secondly, such cars encouraged the driver to go faster than he would in most

This Zinnober red UK 1985 528i has a two-way sunroof, and used to have TRX rims. (Courtesy Peter Thorpe)

other vehicles. Put these together and you have an increased possibility of a larger number of folks getting into trouble.

Apart from road testers and buyers getting caught out by Jekyll and Hyde changes in suspension behaviour, noises were coming from another important sector. ETRTO, a body representing European tyre manufacturers, was adding its two cents to the issue of suspension behaviour at the limit. ETRTO set a ceiling for maximum camber change, beyond which the tyre maker wouldn't be responsible

for the response of its tyres. There was more than a little pressure for change and, to its credit, BMW responded.

DOUBLE PIVOT & TRAC-LINK SUSPENSION
For the front suspension this meant adoption of the double pivot front suspension first seen on the new 1977 BMW E23 7 Series. The customary style for front MacPherson strut suspension is to have the lower A arm or single lower arm braced with an angled link to set the base of the strut.

In any case, the base of the strut is retained by just one ball joint. BMW's spin – no pun intended – on the status quo was to utilise two positioning links, one lateral plus another angled forward. Each link was attached to the strut with its own ball joint.

This geometrical piece of lateral thinking allowed the engineers to stave off the expected MacPherson strut trait of nose dive on braking without sacrificing the presence of an acceptable roll centre position. Anyone who can recall the old E3, 2500/2800/3.0 will attest to the annoying pitching encountered in the normal MacPherson strut arrangement. Perhaps even more importantly, the double pivot front end permitted BMW engineers to come up with a changeable scrub radius, one that varies as the steering wheel is turned. During cornering the double pivot front would produce a large scrub radius to aid steering returnability. At the straight ahead position there would be a smaller scrub radius which would fight off self steering effects when a flat tyre arises on one side, or during braking with the front wheels on two different surfaces.

Getting a car on two different surfaces can generate unequal forces pulling the car in a particular direction. BMW's double pivot front was probably a better choice in this area than the zero offset geometry used by Daimler-Benz on its W116 S class. The S class' ability to deal with the unequal forces depended greatly on the condition of its steering box. A worn steering box greatly impaired straightline directional stability. The good news for the E28 5 Series doesn't stop there, as anything that could be done at the front could be bettered at the back.

The E28 5 Series was the first BMW to receive the revised semi-trailing arm rear suspension incorporating Trac-Link. In this respect it was the guinea pig for a system that would be added to the 6 and 7 Series from the start of 1983. The 6 series was really kept in the dark, since as late as 1982 it possessed neither the double pivot front or the modified semi-trailing arm rear. The front suspension revisions gave the revised 5s considerable front end grip, but

the transformation at the back was even more spectacular and noticeable. At first the different rear suspension was restricted to the European 528i, but eventually filtered down the 5 Series range.

The angle created by the semi-trailing arm axis of rotation and halfshaft centreline was reduced from 20 degrees to 13 degrees. The end result was reduced camber toe in and track change, accompanied by a lower static roll centre. The net product from stopping here would be a more progressive loss of traction at the back, whilst sudden changes in direction, such as those encountered moving through a slalom course, would be less pleasant. To deal with the last problem BMW raised the pivot points for the rear semi-trailing arms. This modification dealt with sudden direction changes whilst containing the annoying squat experienced with a burst of acceleration.

The engineers were still not over the finish line. To combat the trait of independent rear ends jacking up, some track change would be beneficial. The E12 style bushings for the semi-trailing arm attachment points were dumped and replaced with an axially squishier variety. When combined with a supplementary suspension link, nicknamed Trac-Link, the engineering fairy godmother had finished distributing the magic sprinkles and the bimmer suspension picture was back on track. The right suspension movement, in the right direction and to the right degree – well, almost!

Those who have hotted-up E12s will attest to the grip, slip, grip pendulum scenario encountered if

you initially get out of shape. The pendulum action decreases with reduction in momentum. That's assuming the driver manages to catch the slide in the first place. And if not? Well, in that case, you just spin! Then again, you'd have to have been travelling very fast for this to happen. With the E28 there was the same high cornering limit, followed by timely and calmer warnings to desist from high-spirited shenanigans.

The story now involved more neutrality, less experience of line tightening with a suddenly closed throttle. If the character at the wheel didn't know what he was doing, there was a back door to escape through. While circumstances had changed appreciably in some ways, in others they had stayed the same. Testers in America and Europe still felt there was too much variation with the theme. The mild understeer at low speeds still gave way to full blown oversteer at the point of no return. Rex Greenslade, *Motor*'s contemporary technical editor, mentioned how dismayed the BMW engineers appeared when informed that there was still room to curb rear end waywardness.

Martin Hodder also noted how a driver had to back off in the wet, especially at a roundabout, to avoid the risk of loss of traction. So whilst previous tendencies were checked, they weren't eradicated. There is an upside to this story, however. If a car that responds to driver whim with sharp measured changes is what is wanted, this can be at a cost of some untimely, unwanted movements. Start the jelly moving and it doesn't always cease activity on command! Given that the majority of cars are still set

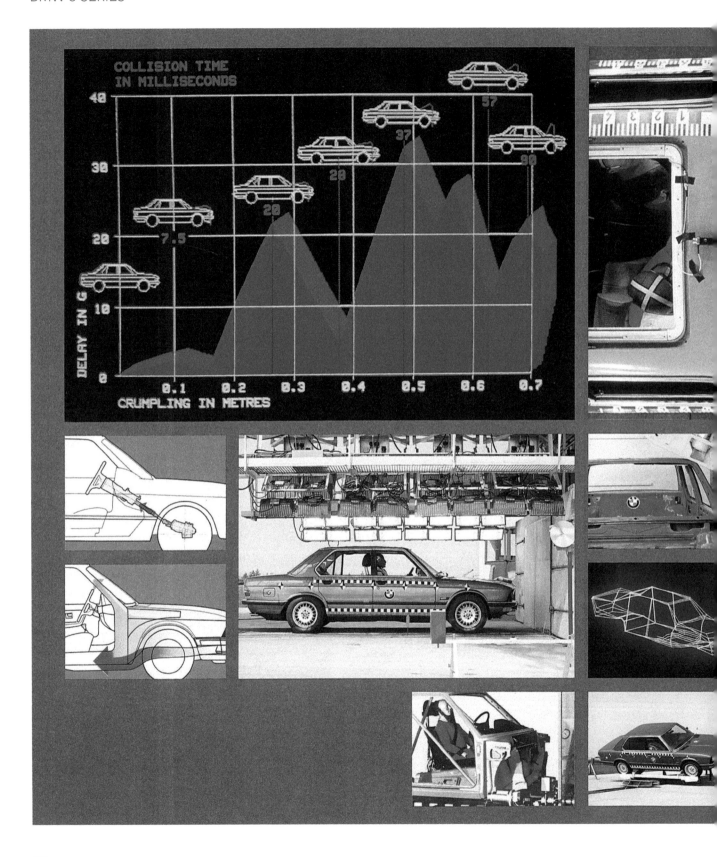

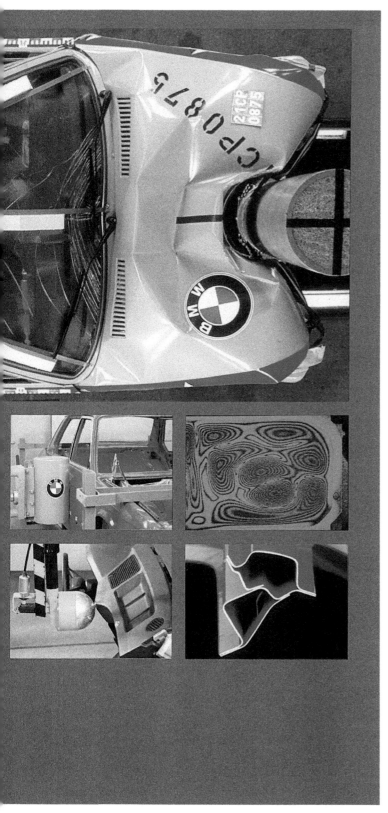

As ever, the E28 5 Series benefited from BMW's study of auto safety. 722,328 E28 5 Series cars were made from 1981 to 1987. (Courtesy BMW)

up to quietly understeer off the road so as to offend nothing but the scenery, the E28's idiosyncrasy may have been an acceptable price to pay.

BMW has never really toed the conventional line in order to garner broad acceptance. Most automakers steer clear of courting extremes for fear of receiving mixed reviews. *R&T* summed up the BMW's unconventional spirit best by saying: "You could imagine the board of directors in Munich dressed as pinstripe conservative as their counterparts in Stuttgart, but with the Bimmer men wearing red underwear and being anxious to get to their motorcycles for an afternoon's ride." BMW's development engineers used to be known for their particular interest and background in motorsport. In a world full of compromise surely it's not unreasonable to expect driver ability to at least be in the same ballpark as that of the car they intend to thread through a few hypothetical alpine switchbacks? To expect any less would be too tough on the car!

ABS – ANTI BLOC SYSTEM
The E28's revised front suspension also had implications for the instalment of anti-lock brakes for the first time on a production 5 Series. Anti-lock brakes, or ABS (Anti Bloc System), had been waiting in the wings for a long time. Back in the sixties the Jensen Interceptor FF, a four wheel drive super express using Ferguson style four wheel drive, had a Dunlop Maxaret ABS system. However, if the system discussed is computer controlled and operates on all four wheels, then we must once again look to the R&D gnomes in West Germany.

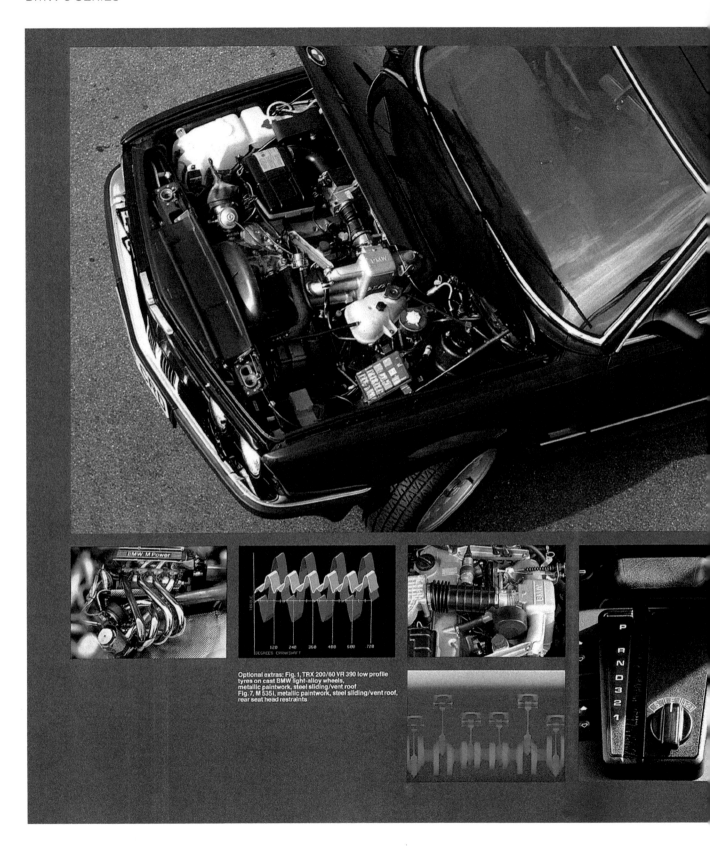

Optional extras: Fig. 1, TRX 200/60 VR 390 low profile
tyres on cast BMW light-alloy wheels,
metallic paintwork, steel sliding/vent roof
Fig. 7, M 535i, metallic paintwork, steel sliding/vent roof,
rear seat head restraints

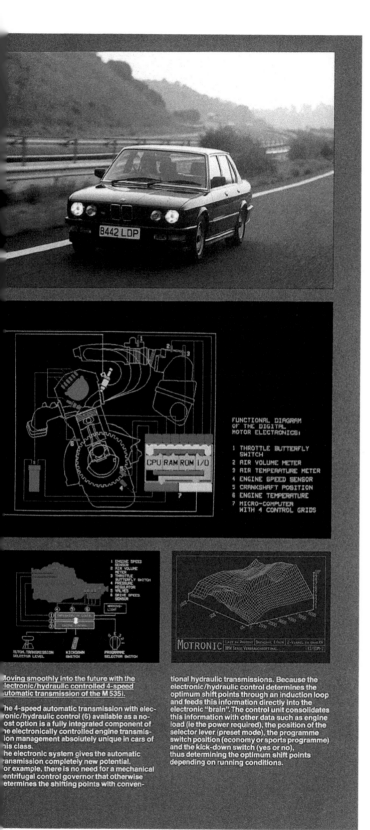

Bosch Motronic injection, TRX rims/tyres, and a switchable electro/hydraulic four-speed autobox were just some of the tricks the 5 Series had in the mid '80s. (Courtesy BMW)

FUNCTIONAL DIAGRAM OF THE DIGITAL MOTOR ELECTRONICS:

1 THROTTLE BUTTERFLY SWITCH
2 AIR VOLUME METER
3 AIR TEMPERATURE METER
4 ENGINE SPEED SENSOR
5 CRANKSHAFT POSITION
6 ENGINE TEMPERATURE
7 MICRO-COMPUTER WITH 4 CONTROL GRIDS

CPU RAM ROM I/O

1 ENGINE SPEED SENSOR
2 AIR VOLUME METER
3 THROTTLE BUTTERFLY SWITCH
4 PRESSURE REGULATOR
5 VALVES
6 DRIVE SPEED SENSOR

AUTOM. TRANSMISSION SELECTOR LEVER   KICKDOWN SWITCH   PROGRAMME SELECTOR SWITCH

MOTRONIC

Moving smoothly into the future with the electronic/hydraulic controlled 4-speed automatic transmission of the M535i.

The 4-speed automatic transmission with electronic/hydraulic control (6) available as a no-cost option is a fully integrated component of the electronically controlled engine transmission management absolutely unique in cars of this class.
The electronic system gives the automatic transmission completely new potential. For example, there is no need for a mechanical centrifugal control governor that otherwise determines the shifting points with conven-

tional hydraulic transmissions. Because the electronic/hydraulic control determines the optimum shift points through an induction loop and feeds this information directly into the electronic "brain". The control unit consolidates this information with other data such as engine load (ie the power required), the position of the selector lever (preset mode), the programme switch position (economy or sports programme) and the kick-down switch (yes or no), thus determining the optimum shift points depending on running conditions.

In the late sixties an electronic system was developed by Teldix, controlled by Telefunken and Bendix, at a cost of 15,000,000 (1971) deutschmarks. Teldix worked with a number of car companies, most notably Daimler-Benz. In the United States Ford introduced an electronic anti-lock setup that operated just on the rear brakes.

American full-size saloons had been using front wheel power assisted disc brakes for a number of years by then. However, drum brakes were still common as far as the rear axle went. It was the rear drums that were more likely to lock up in a panic stop, so it made sense to have the anti-lock work on these. There was some logic in this partial approach to taming tail slides and loss of traction; such a system could be seen on the 1970 Lincoln. Having a computer controlled anti-lock system ready for a European showroom model took longer.

Anti-lock brakes were in evidence in racing, as used by the hard charging Hans Stuck jr in the early seventies with the factory racing CSL coupé in the European Touring Car Championship, but, for various reasons, its introduction into series production stalled. There was the 1973/4 energy crisis, plus the world recession that slowed car sales. More importantly, there were technical bugs to be eliminated from the electronic ABS system. These were early days for using computers in cars. The use of a computer to govern the air/fuel mixture had just begun. Using a computer to keep the braking system on the margin before locking took quite some doing. With racing, the volume

The E28 and E30 were more competitively priced than their 1970s UK market predecessors. However, standard equipment was still modest compared with non Mercedes rivals. (Courtesy BMW)

of just 0.40 inches, avoiding excess steering corrections when braking on two different surfaces, was of prime importance in allowing ABS to be introduced. Given that the E28 5 Series shared the double pivot front end, what worked for the E23 7 Series would also work on the revised 5 Series.

Technically, the E28's braking system was a step backwards from the system used on the older E12. All E12s had a conventional vacuum-assisted power braking setup. The M30 equipped variants in the E28 range used a high pressure hydraulic system, as first seen on the 1977 7 Series.

The 525i and 528i E28 versions retained the E12's twin circuit braking system, where one circuit covered all four wheels and the remaining circuit took care of the front wheels. The lower powered 518 and 520i, with rear drum brakes, had the retrogressive diagonally split circuit setup. It must be noted that these were early days in the E28's life. The technical advantages in suspension, brakes and other features enjoyed by the 528i would filter down through the E28 range in the years to come.

SYSTEM TRX MICHELIN – WHEELS & TYRES

It would be appropriate at this point to say a few words about the type of alloy rim you could have on your 5 Series BMW. Tyre and rim technology never remains static and, for the eighties, the

of computer units is low, and the manufacturer can keep a close watch over quality. So, up until the late seventies, full computer controlled ABS remained in the racing arena.

In 1978 the Mercedes W116 S class became available with ABS as an option for the first time. It cost 2500 pounds sterling, about the same as a family-sized European Ford Escort! BMW introduced ABS on the 1980 745i; it had been a long time coming, to say the least.

The 7 Series-derived, double pivot front suspension helped the use of ABS. The ability of being able to have a small scrub radius theme was one of integration. In the sense that the whole is often greater than the sum of its parts, the tyre and rim combination could be used to bring greater benefits for all aspects of car behaviour. Even in the early eighties alloy rims were hardly as common as they are today. In the seventies they were rarer still. BMW and Daimler-Benz usually offered a single corporate style in the 14-inch format to suit their ranges. In BMW's case, this entailed the Alpina style turbine rim in either 13- or 14-inch form.

For the eighties the world met the TRX phenomenom. If a tyre and rim could be designed with each other in mind, then the full advantages of the contemporary radial tyre could be achieved. This entailed a specially sized metric rim being teamed up with a metric sized Michelin tyre. The objective was to achieve superior handling while maintaining an acceptable ride. The package was also designed to give the driver greater control in a high speed blow out. Ford used the TRX system on the Mustang between 1979 and 1985; Ferrari also used it, and even BMW gave it a try.

The TRX rim was effectively the largest sized rim a manufacturer could get its hands on. It offered the opportunity to fit larger brake rotors and play around with suspension geometry. As far as the E28 5 Series went, the rim was 390mm by 165mm. The traditional Alpina style, 20 spoke and BBS basket weave design continued for a time.

In action the TRX system had advantages and disadvantages, although isolating the effect the tyre and rim combination had on the E28 was difficult, given its revised suspension design. Testers mentioned that, in spite of the low profile and wide section, the combination delivered good comfort along with excellent transient response.

The consensus of opinion was that the TRX package was lacking in outright grip, making recording short stopping distances in brake tests difficult. Of somewhat greater concern was the issue of cost and availability, as the Michelin tyre and rim were not cheap. Plus, if you had TRX rims then you had to use the metric tyre; nothing else would fit!

In the years since the TRX days, getting replacement tyres has become difficult. In defence of 'system TRX,' it must be said that it was the best overall solution available at the time.

Alpina's 245bhp B9 saloon used the E28 5 Series as its basis. (Courtesy Francois Gaignaux)

6

GIZMOS, GADGETS, AND ... DIESELS?

The early eighties were very different to the preceding decade and the E28 seemed at odds with this scenario, given its visual similarity to the E12 of the early seventies. Back then, BMW and Daimler-Benz were in a similar boat with their E12 5 Series and W116 S class. Both cars were launched in 1972, before the first fuel crisis. Both European cars, albeit luxury models, they were designed with high fuel prices in mind. However, the designers couldn't have foreseen the overnight quadrupling of fuel prices that was about to happen. The 1956 Suez crisis was becoming a distant memory by this stage, and all were caught unprepared.

It could be that both models would have turned out rather differently if the imminent constraints could have been factored in. As things stood, both were well designed cars which made it through the seventies in a commercially successful manner. It is well documented that the E23 7 Series went back to the drawing board due to the rise in world oil prices. British Leyland was forced to rethink its planned large executive cruiser, which resulted in the simpler RT1 and the production SD1. What started out as a rival for

the Mercedes 300 SEL 6.3 became a smaller, simpler, live axle Ferrari Daytona inspired hatchback.

Unlike the British designers of the Rover SD1, David Bache and Spen King, the German designers at BMW and Daimler-Benz were stuck. Their cars were already set in stone and released to the public. However, 1981 would be different. With the E28 5 Series and the W126 S class the designers at the esteemed German companies would have a second bite at the cherry, a chance to offer a different technical solution more in keeping with the present economic climate. They had quite a few tricks up their sleeves which were not limited to weight saving and aerodynamics.

BMW R&D FOR THE 1980s

At BMW intense R&D into technical efficiency was about to bring forth valuable solutions, solutions that would become a major part of BMW models in the coming years. Signs of what was planned were revealed at BMW's Technik Tag, or Technical Day, conferences. These occasions represented a get-together between the motoring press and BMW's R&D boffins, and gave an opportunity to discuss the current automotive scene and the near future. Such conferences took place in 1978 and 1981, and the latter event was very important as it occurred on the eve of the E28's release. These meetings give a good idea of how BMW's strong engineering and development backgrounds have contributed to its present success.

A key area of concern was discovering the best path to economical driving. In the seventies, fuel economy vacuum gauges were all the rage; these devices led to the belief that, to save on fuel, a light foot was necessary at all times. However, this myth was about to be exploded: Detroit engineers, trying to get good economy EPA figures to slap on showroom car windows, and BMW personnel soon found that the road to fuel savings lay in a heavy foot!

The reasons were quite logical. Keep the engine turning over relatively slowly to avoid frictional losses; changing up early sounds fine, but why a heavy foot? Simply to reduce internal pumping losses. The engine has to fight hard to suck air past a barely open throttle plate, which is the case with light pressure, so don't baby the gas pedal: in short, avoid high revs and go heavy on the accelerator pedal. BMW worked out that the most effective and economical way to get a car up to speed, the time when the majority of gas guzzling occurs, is to push the pedal three quarters of the way to the floor and change up at 2000rpm.

Another chief topic at Technical Days was the variable displacement engine. Everyone was trying to figure out how to combine big engine poke with little engine economy. When the fuel crisis hit hard the first time, and back

New alloy rims, C pillar air extraction vent and rear lamp treatment apart, many felt that the E28 looked very similar to the older E12. (Courtesy Kevin Ellis)

During the reign of the jelly mould in the early '80s, the E28's upright styling was criticised. However, such arguments died away as the decade progressed. (Courtesy Kevin Ellis)

Power seats were a new feature for the E28 5 Series. The control buttons were located on the handbrake console between the front seats. (Courtesy Chris Baker)

Interior wood trim was out, and BMW claimed the new E28 5 Series had more rear legroom than the older E3 saloon! (Courtesy Kevin Ellis)

in the Suez crisis days, too, small economical cars became instantly popular. The trouble was that buyers were not at all pleased with the meagre performance and comfort small, fuel conserving vehicles gave. There had to be a better compromise out there. Well, many – like Ford and General Motors – turned to the turbocharger. Use waste exhaust gases forced under pressure, along with an enriched fuel mixture, to make a small motor act like a big one when necessary.

The other option was to have a relatively large, normally-aspirated motor and use only as much of it as absolutely necessary: the essence of the variable displacement engine. Cadillac division became a famous exponent with its V8-6-4 motor. Utilising valve gear disengagement, this motor tried to save on fuel and increase operating efficiency by working as much as possible in V6 and V4 modes, calling on V8 trim only when

full acceleration was required. Working with the partial use, high load concept, BMW created its own spin on variable displacement with a special 323i.

Using the E21 323i as the basis for the project, BMW engineers put forward a variable displacement version of the standard 2.3-litre straight six that did without valve gear disengagement. Most of the time the 323i would be operating using just three of its six pots, with fuel feed to the dormant cylinders

interrupted when engine load was light. Exhaust gases would be directed from the operating cylinders to the sleeping chambers. Apart from deriving every last drop of energy from the non-functioning chambers, the warming exhaust gases would maintain combustion chamber temperature in the dormant chambers. This would facilitate refiring when the other three cylinders were brought back online.

BMW engineers chose to go

as the crow flies and select the technical path of least resistance. The experimental motor retained its Bosch K-jetronic mechanical injection and used a set of baffles to channel the exhaust gases to the sleeping chambers. There was no need for the complex and possibly troublesome valve disengagement. The added bonus was that the variable displacement BMW engine spent more time in partial mode operation than the Caddy V8-6-4 engine. That was the whole point of the exercise, to run part of the engine at high load to maximise efficiency. We can now proceed to the concept of valued mileage.

SERVICE INTERVAL – SI – INDICATOR SYSTEM

For so very long the majority of car servicing has been based on either a fixed time or distance, and yet it is well recognised that driving patterns and driving style play a big part in looking after a car. Frequent starts and short trips are harder on an automobile than a single start and long trip where the driver can maintain a set speed for long periods. It is also easier to get an engine started in a warm climate compared to a freezing one. In the interests of achieving better results, BMW went about developing its concept of valued mileage and service interval (si) indicator system for 1981.

Introduced on the 1981 European range of E28 5 Series cars, the si indicator system freed BMW owners from the existing mandatory 7500km service interval pattern. As mentioned in a contemporary BMW advert, when starting the car, the driver was greeted with a brief but spectacular light show. A computer,

receiving information from engine bay sensors, would work out the optimum service interval based on average journey length, mileage, coolant temperature and engine rpm. It took the guesswork out of when a service was necessary. The computer's considered opinion was relayed to the driver through a series of coloured light emitting diodes (LEDs).

A fully serviced car would show a full complement of five green lights, with each gradually going out as time and mileage accumulated. When all 5 green LEDs had gone out a yellow light would come on, telling the owner that it was time to book a service. A further three red LEDs chastised the owner if he was tardy in arranging a service! At first, the system was restricted to the new 5 Series. However, as 1983 wore on, it made its way to all other model ranges.

From this point, BMW owners became well versed in the BMW jargon of inspection one and inspection two dealer duties, which simply amounted to alternating between a minor oil change and a more involved full-scale service. Once complete, the BMW garage would use its service tool to reset the indicator system and the owner would be greeted by five green lights once again.

In 1971/2, BMW introduced its fusebox-located service diagnosis connector. When hooked up to the Sun diagnosis module in the BMW workshop, a speedy health check could be performed on the car. A decade on, the si system was taking convenience of ownership and motoring cost minimisation to the next level.

There were teething problems with the system. Early cars

seemed to require more frequent servicing than was necessary. *What Car?*, when commenting in a secondhand survey on the E30 3 Series in 1987, noted that some owners had completely bypassed the si electronic board and gone back to fixed interval checks. Fortunately, this state of play seemed to improve with time; later models held true to the promise of longer service intervals and reduced costs for motorists that didn't push their cars hard and did long trips at a steady speed. *Autocar* did a long-term test on the E28 518i back in 1986, and mentioned that the si system had permitted its car to go beyond the expected fixed mileage service points.

Following on from the si indicator system was BMW's dash display of fuel consumption, a more sophisticated version of the humble vacuum gauge. In the bottom half of the rev counter's circular face was a clockwise-moving fuel consumption display. The device based its information on the time the engine's fuel injectors remained open when supplying fuel. For once, the driver would have an accurate reflection of fuel usage as he accelerated.

On the reverse of the E28's instrument display unit are printed circuit boards which electronically relay readouts for speed, engine revolutions, coolant temperature, etc, via a multiplug connecter to a computer. The instruments were still sourced from VDO, but we have moved on from the days when readouts on a car's performance are derived solely from mechanical instruments. Beyond this, BMW redesigned the 5 Series dash and interior for the eighties. The E28 represented the first time a 5 Series was brought into line with BMW practice of having a dashboard with the major controls grouped together and angled towards the driver.

The idea of grouping controls and having an angled dashboard was first seen on the 1972 BMW Turbo gullwing show car. The idea was first put into effect on the 1975 E21 3 Series, and was finally incorporated on the 5 Series with the new E28 range of 1981/2. *Autocar*'s Nick Carter mentioned how many manufacturers had tried to copy this successful piece of architecture, especially Ford of Europe with the 1982 Sierra, without totally succeeding. With the new BMW interior it was another case of there being change, but not that much.

Motor's Rex Greenslade likened the situation to visiting your tailor for a new quality suit: the new one fits the same and feels the same, but subtle changes in style reflect current fashion. Apart from the restyled, more flowing dash, there were many adjustable square shaped fresh air vents, new door trims, seats and detail changes in materials. Overall it looked pretty much like the E12's interior. However, on closer inspection one can see that, with the exception of the stereo speaker covers, the designers had changed just about everything. As a side note, interior trim, like seats and door trim, are interchangeable between the E12 and E28. Some owners have updated their E12s with E28 dash and interior fittings.

BMW's 1959 V8 model catalogue, called "The great European eight-cylinders," said that at 30,000DM the sexy 507

For most European buyers, the expensive E28 184bhp 528i was the 5 Series flagship model. As the final reverse slope grille 'shark' BMW, the E28's classic status is assured. (Courtesy Derin Oloyede)

The 528i id badge was something 316 owners could only dream of. No need to exercise the badge delete option on this baby! (Courtesy Derin Oloyede)

sportscar: "incl. complete heating and air conditioning system." At the same time, Mercedes offered a/c on its luxury 300 series. However, both were dealer fitted systems. The first factory fitted a/c from BMW, was on the 1968 BMW E3 saloons and E9 coupes, with Mercedes their 1963 600 V8. The first US BMW with standard a/c was the 1973 3.0S, and in markets that got it, the 1974 3.3L.

The 5 Series first gained a factory a/c option for 1974 model year. At the same time a Behr-designed system, whose console controls looked like those on the Behr E3/E9/E12 units, became available on US 2002s. However, on the 2002 it was a dealer installed unit. The

For the E28, the E12's whole centre section was carried over. So, contrary to BMW claims, interior space was pretty similar. (Courtesy Derin Oloyede)

With less weight than the identically powered 628CSi/728i, the 184 horse 528i allowed the 2.8-litre M30 to excite! (Courtesy Derin Oloyede)

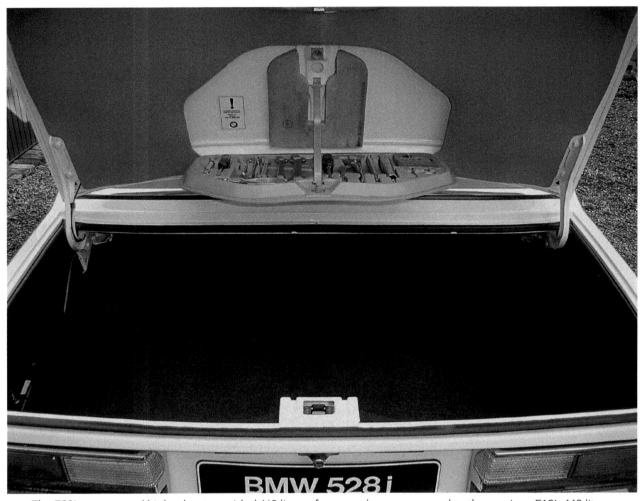

The E28's squarer and higher boot provided 460 litres of cargo volume, compared to the previous E12's 440 litres. (Courtesy Derin Oloyede)

E21 3 Series was the first small BMW with factory a/c. 1978-81 5 Series had their HVAC controls integrated, so a/c came on when the temp dial was turned to the blue sector. So, you couldn't run the a/c and heater simultaneously to create dry, warm air, as in 1974-77. In the E3-E28 era, having a/c meant losing the console cubby hole.

Early 1982-83 E28 5 Series restored the chance of running the heater and a/c together. You just hit the big snowflake button when the temp dial was in the red sector. However, American customers complained of poor a/c performance in the E28, not realising you had to close the sliders to the full circle close position to shut off outside air. That is, to put the a/c into recirc mode. E28s with a/c had different shaped dashboard consoles.

To overcome the problem, BMW rigged 1984 model year E28s with a/c so that when you hit the snowflake button, the fresh air vent doors audibly closed. The job was done by electric servo motors behind the dashboard. As a result, unlike the E30 3 Series, the E28 never got a recirc button! It solved a problem US E12 owners had too, with many not knowing you had to manually close the sliders to get recirc mode. So used were US owners to HVAC control panels written in long hand, where a push of a lever did things automatically.

E12 5 Series had early and late style a/c consoles, with the change-over occurring for 1978 model year. Many detail 5 Series changes were made to bring BMW's midsizer into line with

A non-a/c centre console in this automatic 528i. The E28 was the first 5 Series with BMW's famous divided/angled dashboard. (Courtesy Derin Oloyede)

the new E23 7 Series. However, the E28 kept its dashboard look constant throughout its 1981-87 run. The 5 Series shared a/c hardware, like the evaporator core, with the E24 6 Series. The E3, E9 and E21 shared the same evaporator core. BMW and Behr cooling engineers, partly developed the 6 Series' a/c in Arizona and Texas. In February 1979, *Road & Track* said the 528i's HVAC "all seems to work well now ...

The first BMW with climate control was the E23 7 Series. The E28 5 Series never got that, but did receive an optional auxiliary fuel burning heater, which you could preset via a LCD display. In the E3 to E28 era, a TX valve on the evap core regulated refrigerant flow. A R134a calibrated valve, PAG oil for the a/c compressor, new refrig lines, R134a drier flask and parallel flow condenser are necessary for R12 to R134a conversions.

One interior fitting notable by its absence was wood trim. The E12 had real wood trim, but the E28 had nothing. During the period under consideration, wood was simply out of fashion, in Europe, at any rate. Unlike its sixties predecessor, the CS coupé, the 1976 E24 6 series, didn't feature wood. Like the later E28 5 Series, it simply had high quality, textured, energy absorbing black plastic. *C&D* noted that it gave a glimpse of tomorrowland, and mentioned that it imparted an expensive aura closer to Lear Jet, NASA space control expensive than English club plush or American faux wood expensive. Even Jaguar followed this changing fashion when it introduced the 1975 XJS, which

The 1985 model year E28 M535i reached the UK slightly before the M5. The former car was well known for its M Technic bodykit and disc style metric alloys. (Courtesy Gary Langton)

The optional electro-hydraulic ZF 4HP22 switchable four-speed autobox had three programs with altered shift point patterns. (Courtesy Gary Langton)

didn't have any wood either. Of course, myth and aficionado pressure saw to it that a few two-by-four planks were included down the track, an example of contemporary practice and myth as opposing forces.

Blacked out and dechromed trim was another eighties fashion statement. Familiar designs were stripped of their chrome to update their appeal. The E28 hung onto some exterior brightwork, much more than contemporary rivals possessed, but received blacked out centre pillars and door handles. Another departure came in the shape of the inside door opening mechanism. For years, BMWs had a release handle that was operated by putting a hand down through the front armrest and squeezing.

Shown in New Zealand, the M535i's character was a good match for the yuppie/boy racer era of the 1980s. However, like the E12 M535i, it was affordably priced for a BMW. (Courtesy Peter Crow)

This time around, the M535i had the 10:1 CR Motronic, small bore/long stroke 3430cc I6. It still made 218bhp, but was more frugal than the old M90. (Courtesy Peter Crow)

Without the bodykit, the model was simply denoted 535i. Here, aftermarket ROH 16-inch rims have replaced the original metric TRX items. (Courtesy Peter Crow)

This E28 M535i made its way to the States, via the infamous 'gray market.' It still wears its original metric TRX rims. (Courtesy Duke Samouce)

BMW North America didn't much care for the gray market importers, feeling they stole sales from BMW's official upscale models. (Courtesy Duke Samouce)

Apparently this design, on BMWs and some other models, led to a few people accidentally opening the door whilst the car was on the move. The mechanism was replaced by conventional flaps flush with the door trim panel, as seen on the 1977 E23 7 Series.

The E28 obviously enjoyed a number of technical improvements, but was the public at large impressed? The response was mixed; aerodynamics were all the rage in the early eighties and people tended to equate progress with a low drag shape. Donald Kopka, Ford's then vice president, relayed to *Autocar* in 1986 how instrumental aerodynamics were improving the economy of Ford's US car fleet. The European Ford

Sierra also reflected the popularity of low drag thinking – it was a spin-off of the Ford Probe show cars. Audi was also getting in on the act with its windcheating 1982 Audi 100. In fact, Audi was so proud of its car's low drag factor that it had the 0.30 coefficient figure etched onto the rear window glass!

The Ford Sierra and Audi 100 quickly became darlings with the motoring press and technologically motivated buyers. Their futuristic aero bodies were reminiscent of the fifties Citroën DS, even if the mechanicals didn't have the innovation of the French automobile. Anyway, it all sparked noises that BMW's boxy, upright product line was dated and obviously resided somewhere

in dullsville! Audi couldn't resist rubbing BMW's corporate nose in it with its 1984 advert comparing the 125bhp 100 2.1 and the 125bhp BMW 520i. Much was made of the fact that the Audi's low drag permitted it to record a 125mph top speed, significantly higher than that of the 520i.

Audi also made great fanfare of the 100's gradual loss of speed when the driver lifted off the accelerator pedal on the high speed banked test bowl. The ability of the Audi 100 to pass through the air with ease was the closest thing to perpetual motion. This last claim was ironic, given the problem Audi was about to experience in the US market. As reported by *60 Minutes*, not only could some

Audi 100s maintain speed with the foot off the accelerator, they could actually increase speed, too. There were more than just a few reported incidents of automatic Audi 5000s, the US Audi 100, spontaneously picking up speed without driver input.

It was a public relations disaster with a major negative effect on US Audi sales. In fact, it took the 1995 arrival of the A4 to get Audi back on track in the States. That was 1995; back in 1988, Audi was left with a new car stockpile over three times the size of the trade average. As AMC's Gerald C Meyer told *Fortune* magazine in July 1979: "That's no way to run a business." Audi sales were falling off in major European volume markets by 1987/1988. In contrast, Volvo, with its angular 740/760 range, and BMW with the E28, both strong enough to resist climbing on the fashion bandwagon, did better business in the States.

Somehow these allegedly dated-looking designs had a longer shelf life than the cutting edge brigade of fresh ingredients! While it may have seemed short-sighted to have bucked the low drag trend, the sales figures show that, between 1974 and 1985, BMW was able to increase sales in North America in each successive year. It wasn't all plain sailing for BMW but, vorsprung durch technik or not, it was BMW that had the better image at the end of the eighties. Audi was the one left amalgamating the 100/200 shell with the new 3.6-litre V8 in an attempt to boost its buyer appeal.

THE ETA 5 SERIES
However, even BMW couldn't afford to sit back and ignore trends and preferences. Interest in fuel economy intensified in Europe after the second fuel crisis. The low drag Audi 100 was one solution, and BMW was working on a response. The answer was the thoughtful 525e, a deep approach to getting the last ounce of energy from petroleum distillate. It represented a roadgoing model encompassing what BMW had learned concerning reducing internal pumping and frictional losses. The 525e, where e stood for ETA, the Greek letter engineers use to denote efficiency, was released in early 1983. At the heart of the package was a 2.7-litre version of BMW's baby M60 small six.

The goal was big torque at low revs, and in Europe the concept was taken to its ultimate conclusion by offering 11-to-1 compression for models produced up to 1986. Bosch DME and a tall final drive promised miserly fuel figures, and these were indeed realised. The relatively large-engined 5 Series almost matched the fuel economy of the much lighter 1.8-litre 518i as an automatic! This was, perhaps, the 525e's greatest achievement; excellent, attainable fuel consumption in a world car specification. Sure, the Audi 100 2.1 had great fuel figures, but not all markets would have liked the tall gearing, manual transmission and small displacement solution necessary to achieve them.

The BMW 525e could give buyers in a number of markets the benefits of reduced thirst. At 2.7 litres it nicely undercut the 2.8-litre limit affecting much of continental Europe, most notably France. As an automatic car with a flat torque curve, it was also eminently suited to the North American market. A car for all seasons? Well, not quite, but in an era when the world car concept was on the tip of every car industry heavyweight's tongue, the 525e came closer to this ideal than other models that consciously sought this objective. How did BMW do it? Simply by following the high load, low rpm principle to the letter!

Unlike the usual BMW pattern of maximum power and torque developed at high rpm, the 525e featured a lowly 125 horses at 4250rpm, and a healthy 177 pounds per foot at a mere 3250rpm. Lightweight valvegear was utilised to limit frictional losses, and, as a result, the redline was set at a very low 4750rpm. At this point fuel supply to the engine shut off. Everything was maximised for high load partial use. The standard automatic, with tall overdrive fourth, actually contributed to the economy picture. Shift points could be adjusted to facilitate gear changing at the optimal 2000rpm.

With the automatic it would be even easier to recreate the economy shuffle of three quarter throttle and 2000rpm shifting. Aside from mile-stretching economy, the ETA concept made for remarkably refined and civilised touring; at 60mph a mere 1600rpm were dialed up on the tach. Refinement, economy, good performance for an automatic – how could the 525e lose? The trouble was that in Britain, and some other markets where BMWs have always been pushed as upmarket, high-performance cars, this model didn't fit in. BMW, and rivals, found that British buyers were not into dishing out more dough to save fuel in an executive car.

At least that was the case in

the early to mid eighties: with fuel prices increasing in the late nineties, British buyers were more concerned with economy in every market segment. However, stripped out base models and versions with a leaning towards economy were better suited to continental European markets. For Britain the idea of a BMW that cost more but delivered less outright performance had a touch too much lateral thinking. In advertising the revised and expanded BMW 5 Series range in late 1984, encompassing the new 518i and M535i, BMW made great claims concerning improved fuel efficiency.

The advert claim was true, the new M535i did have the same average fuel consumption as a 1978, 1.8-litre BMW. Improved aerodynamics, weight saving, engine management and taller gearing had achieved impressive gains with similar corporate hardware. However, in Britain, such advertising copy largely fell on deaf ears. When testing the new M535i for *Motor* magazine, Peter Frater mentioned that the British owner wealthy enough to purchase the M535i wouldn't be particularly concerned about fuel efficiency ...

It partially explains the difference in offered versions between continental Europe and Britain. On the Continent the idea of a large price tag on a Daimler-Benz S class turbo diesel was quite normal, but British S class buyers would have been more at home with a petrol, V8-powered equivalent. So whilst the 525e was technically interesting and admired by motoring journalists, it didn't generate large sales in Britain.

The ETA concept had greater value in the contemporary North American market. A fuel-efficient petrol powerplant able to contribute to that market's tightening fleet economy average never went to waste.

In Britain, where Audi was cultivating a great image from the Quattro drivetrain and low drag shape, the ETA concept gave technology conscious buyers something to talk about. BMW could also point to the inherited Active Check Control readout panel mounted just behind the rearview mirror. First seen on the higher 6 and 7 Series BMWs, this electronic pad gave a quick health update regarding various vital fluids. With the E28 the gadget became even more active with a dash light coming on to inform of any trouble, less driver input brought forth more information.

Something that was even more likely to impress friends was the incorporation of BMW's trip computer on the E28. It was scaled down when compared to the full 15 function monster on the big brother 7, but, at 10 functions including trip time, average fuel economy and an alert for the temperature at which black ice can form, it was still a little electronic marvel. *R&T* even said it could beat up an Apple II! Such electronic items not only aided the driver, but also improved BMW's commercial standing. In Europe – where having the latest whatever takes on even greater importance – such gadgetry kept BMW's existing product line fresher for longer, until all new model ranges could be released.

THAT OIL BURNING 524TD

Diesels were also one of BMW's winning cards in this era. Goaded by the fuel crisis, even performance-centred BMW couldn't ignore the oil burner's quality of mile stretching economy. Britain's *CAR* mentioned that the idea of a diesel BMW in the early seventies would have been unthinkable, but these weren't the early seventies. Chief engine designer Karlheinz Lange saw to it that BMW proceeded with the development of the petrol M60 baby six into a diesel powerplant. In direct contrast to the kneejerk response to the fuel crisis of some manufacturers, trying to speedily convert existing petrol units into diesel equivalents, the BMW diesel had more preparation. Many still recall the tales of woe associated with GMs' diesel conversion of the 350 Chevy small block. Many Oldsmobile buyers were displeased with the poor reliability of the 350 diesel.

The secret of BMW's success was a specially developed cylinder head, which avoided the usual compromises made concerning glow plug location and porting. The engine was manufactured in Austria by diesel specialist Steyr, and the BMW model it was fitted to was the 1983 524td. Billed as the world's fastest diesel, the 524td had 115bhp and at 48bhp per-litre it out-punched every automotive diesel around. The version was offered for the remainder of the E28's life, and was temporarily joined in 1986 by the normally-aspirated 524d. It was all part of BMW's plan to give European buyers three options in the 120bhp class. Buyers could choose the regular 520i, the ETA petrol 525e or even the oil burning 524td. Three cars with three very different approaches showcasing BMW's wide technical prowess.

Common rail, direct injection turbodiesels have taken off in Europe like wildfire. However, future emissions targets place a question mark over their future. (Courtesy BMW)

After a start that involved assembling Glas automobiles by Praetor Monteerders, what became BMW South Africa had limited success with the E3 2500/2800, before striking gold from 1973 with the E12. BMW South Africa chose to stay with the E12 5 Series shell and incorporate just the mechanical and electronic upgrades that accompanied the E28. From 1982 the Rosslyn factory turned out what was internally referred to as the E12/8, an amalgam of E12 shell and E28 drivetrain, chassis and electronics. Although retaining the restyled 5 Series exterior from 1977, the E12/8 did have the new double pivot front suspension, Trac-Link rear end and other E28 improvements, 23,100 were made.

BMW South Africa chose to tool up for the new E30 3 Series rather than immediately switch to the new 5 Series design. Previously, the 3 Series had not been offered in South Africa due to the market's preference for four-door cars. The new 3 was available in four-door form, so getting that model on stream was of greater priority. The E12/8 was allowed to fight on until the middle of 1985 when the E28 made its belated entry.

The strategy was appropriate for South Africa, where local conditions make the practical aspects of motoring particularly important. It is a country of large distances and relatively poor fuel quality, and the veldt's altitude really saps motor power. Buyers in this market prefer larger, normally-

Höchstleistung unter Druck: Die neue BMW Diesel-Generation mit Common Rail.

Mit dem neuen 525d und dem 530d zeigt BMW eindrucksvoll, wie kraftvoll und dynamisch ein Fahrzeug mit Dieselmotor sein kann. Und wie leise. Schon kurz nach dem Start brillieren die Sechszylinder-Triebwerke in Reihenbauweise mit dezent-ruhigem Lauf. Um dann bereits bei niedrigen Drehzahlen vehement Kraft zu liefern: Im Fall des 530d stehen enorme 390 Nm bereits ab 1750/min zur Verfügung. Dieses Kraftpaket beschleunigt in nur acht Sekunden auf 100 km/h, ist im Dieselverbrauch aber überaus wirtschaftlich. Stichwort: Common Rail. Bei dieser Technik, die über einen gemeinsamen Druckspeicher die einzelnen Einspritzdüsen mit Druck versorgt, kann eine ausgesprochen hohe Leistung realisiert werden. Und das bei vergleichsweise günstigen Verbrauchswerten und einem besonders niedrigen Schadstoffausstoß. Beide Motoren erfüllen die strengen Abgasvorschriften der EU-III-Norm.

Sie müssen schon zweimal hinhören, um den 4-Zylinder-Diesel-Direkteinspritzmotor im 520d als solchen zu erkennen. Mit einem variablen Turbolader, Vierventil-Technik und aufwendiger Geräuschdämmung ausgerüstet, gibt sich der BMW 520d sehr drehmomentstark und legt eine geradezu verblüffende Laufruhe an den Tag. Damit ist die 5er Limousine der ideale Begleiter für lange Reisen und viele Autobahnkilometer. Dank hochpräziser Direkteinspritzung bewegt sich auch der Verbrauch auf denkbar niedrigem Niveau.

aspirated tractable engines with good performance. The efficiency gains the E28 brought, such as new styling with reduced frontal area and a raised bootline for better aerodynamics, were of less importance in this vast country with its high summer temperatures.

1982 528I GROUP A ETCC RACER

For the new international Group A touring car regulations, one had to make at least 5000 units in a year, to homologate a model for racing. Thinking it couldn't get the 635CSi qualified, and thinking Jaguar's XJS wouldn't make it either, BMW backed the new E28 528i as a winning stopgap for 1982.

The spec was a 1035kg 240bhp 528i, riding on 8.5x16in rims shod with Pirelli 245/45 VR16 covers. The team was the Eggenberger/ BMW-supported BMW Italia concern, with the #1 car driver pairing of Umberto Grano and Helmut Kelleners. They won the first five races, and were crowned series champions. A sister BMW Italia 528i won the 1982 Spa 24 Hour race.

The TWR XJS V12 was fast, but a green noobie with teething troubles, and the BMW 528i turned the tables on TWR at Spa. In 1981, a TWR Mazda RX7 had beaten an E12 530i into second place. In 1982, the Spa Enduro was part of the ETCC series, and as per the rest of the season, E28 528i reliability won out over Jag V12 power!

The BMW Italia/Eggenberger 1982 528i ETCC winner. (Courtesy Wouter Melissen)

7

ATLANTIC CROSSING II

Offering something for everyone, this has to be the name of the game in auto life! All things considered, BMW had a successful foray into the North American market with the first 5 Series, but what was it going to do the second time? The game plan was evolution, listening to the needs of buyers, and complying with Federal regulations. The result was a two-pronged approach, well, perhaps a two-and-a-half-pronged approach! Range rationalisation had largely dictated a single US 5 Series variant in the seventies, but things were a mite different now.

First off, CAFE was getting stricter all the time, so fuel economy had to be watched ever more closely, even if the pressure of fuel prices had largely lifted by now. This wasn't that big a deal if you were a large manufacturer with a diverse range of economical and not-so-economical models, as things would even out in the end. But if you were small and largely offered one style of car, it was a bit like being in a planning straightjacket. Cross subsidisation wasn't a game that BMW could easily play because, as *C&D* pointed out, it mostly sold petrol-engined, stick shift-operated go-mobiles. There were no diesel

Caddys or baby econoboxes, like the Opel Isuzu Gemini, purloined from a distant foreign subsidiary to help fudge the economy figures.

HELLO 528E!

BMW couldn't throw its hands up and just accept the gas guzzler tax as a fact of life like Rolls-Royce had, action had to be taken. Hence, the two-and-a-half-pronged attack. A major part of the strategy would be the new for 1982 528e, a very similar animal to the 525e, and the driving force behind the creation of the ETA concept. This replacement for the US 528i would bring home the bacon as far as getting good EPA economy digits were concerned. In spite of the newcomer's 2.7-litre engine, BMW still called the model 528e, recalling the confusion that arose with US buyers when it renamed the 530i as the 528i; this way folks would know that they were looking at a 528i kind of car.

There were three main points of difference between the US 528e and the European 525e. For one, the 528e was going to be the 5 Series hi-seller in the US, whereas the 525e wasn't going to move in big numbers close to home. Secondly, in view of its mission to increase BMW's mpg snatch

The E28s departing for North America still used the extended rubber clad bumpers first seen on 1974 model year US bimmers. (Courtesy Shawn Doughtie)

The 121 horsepower, 2.7-litre ETA motor in the US 528e allowed BMW to expand sales in North America without breaching CAFE. (Courtesy Billy Isbell)

Stateside, the 528e would have a stick shift as standard and be promoted with that box. Thirdly, the 528e didn't have the European version's 11-to-1 compression. Sure, it had a higher compression than the preceding US 528i, in the interests of improved fuel efficiency. However, a diet of 91 octane unleaded meant that the 528e was only going to achieve 9-to-1 compression.

US testers didn't know what to make of this new-age econowunder. After all, the US 528i was quite similar to the European 528i, but this new cat was something else. After years of high rpm BMW variants, this new, high torque, low rpm character was like BMW artificial sweetener. Even the US BMWs could be extended past six grand, but this ETA concept car offered lots of torque lower down and simply lost interest higher up. US testers had hoped that, when the M60 baby six came to America, it would be in the form of a US version 323i, so the economy style ETA approach was something of a disappointment.

To cloud matters even more, the new 2.7 motor actually enjoyed a rev or two, but not too many! As C&D discovered, the 528e had a Jekyll and Hyde personality in reverse. You fed in some throttle, all seemed well and good so you fed in some more. Suddenly, the motor blacked out! In C&D's words you were going "... like Mario Andretti on a snaky two lane and suddenly the engine went into a set of convulsions." Technically, an electronic sentry was shutting off the fuel supply to the motor at the 4750rpm red line to preserve the lightweight valve gear. The fuel shut-off was quite abrupt by today's standards and could be off-putting.

As the 528e was the only 5 sold in the States back in 1982, it's easy to see how US testers got the wrong end of the stick. They had witnessed how the fuel crises and pollution controls had taken their toll on the domestic performance scene, and were used to increasing reliance on foreign makes for the need for speed. Then BMW came forward and said it was adding its weight to the energy picture; it was a case of et tu BMW? Even conservative R&T was moved to warn that it hoped BMW hadn't forgotten the reasons for its past success in the US market ...

The truth was that BMW hadn't forgotten, the 528e was merely the starter in a gourmet three course meal, with the main course arriving in 1983. For now, diners would have to be satisfied with their prawn cocktail! The folks liked the starter, or, in the playful words of BMW North American President Jack Cook, "... some people may not have liked the label, but the dogs loved the dog food." BMW had played all sides and come out a commercial winner yet again! The economy-focused ETA model allowed BMW to sell a greater number of cars Stateside without breaching CAFE and needlessly exposing BMW's cars to the gas guzzler tax.

The lessons learnt and expressed at the Technik Tag conferences concerning high load, low rpm running were put into effect to garner extra US sales. Apart from hitting the bullseye on economove BMW was directing even more effort at meeting particular buyer market needs. As a specialist producer's sales grow, so they edge closer to its competitors on either side of the sales niche, making it necessary to muscle in on their territory for future growth.

C&D was right to mention that 9000 doctors, lawyers and executives would be pleased with the 528e newbie. After all, 1982 saw 5 Series sales double in the States just on 528e power! R&T noted that, in 1982 and the years to follow, BMW purchasers would be increasingly derived from non-core car enthusiasts. Indeed, an eighties 5 Series may have to lock horns with a contemporary Caddy SeVille in the fight for buyers' disposable income. So, while a vocal few despaired over the 528e's lack of outright snap, a far greater number found things to like about the newcomer.

There was the E28's improved air con, the result of putting engineers in a black-on-black US E12 528i and getting them to drive 500 miles long in one day of a Texan summer – ouch! Let us not forget the improved standard equipment encompassing better autosound, power roof and the chance of power seats for the first time on a 5 Series; this really counted in the States. Revised interior and exterior styling and an improved convenience quota rounded out the wider market appeal of 1982's 528e. In spite of the power drop the 528e could still cruise at the then-still illegal 70mph, without either the passengers or the car breaking into a sweat.

Given the circumstances that brought us to 1982, it was fortunate to have any kind of sporty saloon, let alone something of the 528e's caliber. In the mid '70s, C&D listed the Caddy DeVille, Mercury Monarch and Volvo 242

The majority of E28 M5s sold in North America had this tan, two-tone interior. Needless to say, the M5 was only available with a stick shift, perfectly in keeping with its sporting character: anything else would have been simply unthinkable.
(Courtesy Armando Mendoza)

as hypothetical US rivals. By the mid eighties we have a revision of the same basic design going toe-to-toe with a downsized Lincoln Continental, Toyota Cressida and Audi 5000 turbo in *C&D*'s new hypothetical face-off. In view of the changing climate you can't blame BMW for putting its mid ranger on a low calorie diet to keep in step with the stampeding herd.

Unfortunately, there were some new E28 ingredients that were either delayed or never arrived on the US scene. BMW was unable to offer the larger outboard headlamps seen on European variants, but was compelled to adhere to US requirements for equal sized lighting. The service interval indicator system was delayed by falling foul of the EPA's mandatory fixed interval servicing requirement. Forcing fixed intervals meant that the vast majority of cars received tune-up attention with positive flow-ons for pollution levels, but didn't fit in with BMW's new concept of valued mileage.

US testers raised a further question regarding BMW's decision to largely retain the previous model's styling. With an inability to incorporate some of the European E28's technical improvements, it may have been judged commercially dangerous to introduce such a lightly facelifted automobile in such an appearance conscious market. The 1982 sales figures for the 528e put to rest such fears, and on the topic of lost performance? For that we only need view the 1983 US 533i!

The E28 US M5 represented the first time Motorsport had to adapt one of its engines for a market requiring unleaded fuel and a catalytic converter, important groundwork for subsequent M cars. (Courtesy Armando Mendoza)

"Whispering bombs unite! Nuke the meek!" These were the words of *Car and Driver* when meeting the new-for-1983 533i. Due to the restrictions of CAFE, BMW had to check its diary before a performance version of the E28 could be introduced in North America. (Courtesy Eileen Beachell)

BMW had a prototype E12 524Di running by 1978. This became the E28 524td, which caught the tail end of America's diesel interest after the global oil crisis. (Courtesy Chris Hinkel)

THE HI PO 1983 533I

With the bedrock of broad market interests and CAFE requirements met with the friendly 528e, BMW could concentrate on appeasing those individuals with a particular need for speed. To this end BMW had only to reach out for the Federally sanctioned 3.2-litre, 181bhp, M30 six, already used in the larger and heavier 633CSi and 733i, and shoehorn it into the smaller 5 Series structure. Performance was assured and, as noted by *C&D*, it wasn't so much the outright figures recorded but the sheer ease with which they were delivered. As with the 528e, Bosch DME was relied upon to meet performance and economy requirements in an increasingly emissions and economy restricted market.

And the figures? *C&D* managed 0 to 60 in 7.7 seconds, a standing quarter mile of 15.8 seconds and a top end of 128mph. *R&T* recorded 134mph with marginally slower equivalent acceleration times. Of course, all of this was largely academic in what was still 55mph America. Still, after laying out all that cash it was good to know that this four-door, six-cylinder saloon could equal the acceleration times of a 1983 Ford Mustang 5.0 GT, one of the hottest domestic production cars and a major force behind reigniting interest in the pony car scene. If this doesn't impress, think of all the rival big buck four doors that delivered less.

Obviously, there is more to the 533i's repertoire than merely travelling expeditiously in a straight line. The US 533i incorporated the suspension updates introduced on the European E28 528i. US testers were pleased with the 533i's greater neutrality and forgiving nature, even if they had reservations regarding the ease with which the 533i could hang its tail out. This, and the compromises produced by the TRX rim and tyre hardware, were just about the full extent of any criticisms. The 533i still managed to record a large number during the lateral skidpan test, of great importance in the US.

As pollution controls and economy constraints gripped

This US E28 535i, has the 182 horse 3430cc unleaded motor. Zero to sixty in 7.4 seconds, and the E32 750iL rims are a mod! (Courtesy Layton Chauvin)

1985 saw ABS and BMW's 3.5-litre motor become standard fare on the US 535i/635CSi and 735i. (Courtesy Chris Baker)

America, outright acceleration increasingly took a back seat to growing interest in handling. To this effect, it became increasingly common to see all manner of cars slung onto a skidpad to see what lateral g force reading could be registered before the rear end let go. Naturally, the larger the recorded figure, the better. A vehicle able to combine a high reading with excellent ride comfort would be the equivalent of first class honours; with the 533i, recording this double first was never in doubt.

Still, there were remarks about the revised 5's dated attire: "mired in the seventies," were the words chosen by Csaba Csere. In a world increasingly dominated by jello mould Fords and Audis, the BMW's conservative line did raise a few eyebrows. However, it has already been shown that, technically and

The larger alloy rims on this 5 Series accommodate the upgraded rotors (discs) and calipers from the E32 7 Series, handy for hot days at the track! (Courtesy Shawn Doughtie)

practically, the new 528e and 533i were well up to the task and this was reflected in BMW's ability to raise sales from a record 15,000 in 1974 to a new record of 50,000 in 1983. The boxy and reserved styling didn't hold BMW back in increasing its grip on the luxury end of the US market.

The new 5s offered a rare blend of performance, quality, refinement and economy in uncommonly high

The owner is working out a conversion to manual transmission, a popular modification on US BMWs. Even though a high proportion of US bimmers were indeed ordered with a stick, today's enthusiasts are particularly keen on selecting their cogs manually. (Courtesy Shawn Doughtie)

quantities. 1983 marked BMW's ability to convince the EPA that its service interval indicator system wasn't evil, and also marked the return of the 140mph speedo after the darkness of the universal 85mph era. The sun well and trully had its hat on!

THRIFTY 524TD & GAS GUZZLING 535I!

In the following years there was continued and careful improvement. In 1985 the 535i and the 524td arrived, the latter was the half in the two-and-a-half-pronged attack. The diesel's handy introduction helped BMW to replace the 3.2-litre US 5, 6, 7 Series cars with large engined 3.4-litre versions by improving the fleet economy average.

1985 was also the first time that the BMW 3.5-litre motor, actually 3.4 litres by this stage in history, was offered in the US market. This gave us the US 535i, 635CSi and the 735i. All three versions had anti-lock brakes as standard. This was also the first time ABS was offered on a US bimmer. The US 3.4 had 8 to 1 compression, ran on 91 octane unleaded and yielded 182bhp.

US testers were curious about why BMW didn't use a knock sensor in conjunction with the Bosch Motronic to bump up the compression and deliver more of the good stuff. In spite of disappointing paper specs, the US 535i offered more than adequate go. Zero to sixty came up in closer to seven seconds than eight,

In spite of having just 182 horses, versus 218 on the European version, a manual US 535i could still sprint to 60mph in around 7.5 seconds. The moral of the story is to never blindly follow spec sheets. (Courtesy Chris Baker)

and, with a top end of 131mph in overdrive fifth, there was nothing to criticise.

As many have correctly noted, the diesel 5 arrived in the US after

Reaganomics US tax law allowed fancy company cars to be written-off using asset depreciation allowance. This made such grey market purchases rather affordable. Much to BMW North America's chagrin. (Courtesy Hartge)

Steve Dinan started tuning company Dinan in 1979. The business gained attention for its turbo E28s and chassis mods. However, this Dinan E28 has an M88/3 motor. (Courtesy Scottie Sharpe)

Hartge's 240 horse 3.5-litre I6 was even inserted into the E21 3 Series! All tempting automotive grey market morsels.
(Courtesy Hartge)

The US spec S38 DOHC 24-valve 3.5 six was the first pollution-controlled cat motor done by BMW Motorsport. However, this S38 has been hopped-up into a 4-litre turbo. (Courtesy Ken Hawkins)

the diesel boom in the States had passed. Its role lay in improving BMW's economy average, allowing it to offer spicier US models. Up to this point BMW North America was battling the infamous 'gray market' importers. There were buyers in North America willing to shell out big bills to obtain luscious forbidden Euro fruit, like the 323i, 745i turbo and M535i. If a more adventurous US line-up was on hand, sales wouldn't be lost to the gray market.

The 524td sold for $750 less than a 528e, and was a great way to boost overall sales without getting into a slanging match with diesel gurus Daimler-Benz. BMW was right in judging that there was still a market in pollution control,

economy seeking seventies and eighties North America for sprightly petrol powered BMWs.

So this was where the lion's share of effort went. BMW also sold the 524td's engine to Ford for use in the Lincoln LSC Continental Mark VII. It was a humbling experience for a Detroit giant to have to go to a small German manufacturer and an Austrian diesel specialist to get a decent diesel that worked.

Previously, BMW had had just one US 5 representative, now it had several to suit different and ever-changing US tastes. A case where you couldn't kill two birds with one stone! If BMW went narrow, the only dead turkey would have been BMW.

The M5 – never before has such a little tag meant so much to so many! (Courtesy James Nelson)

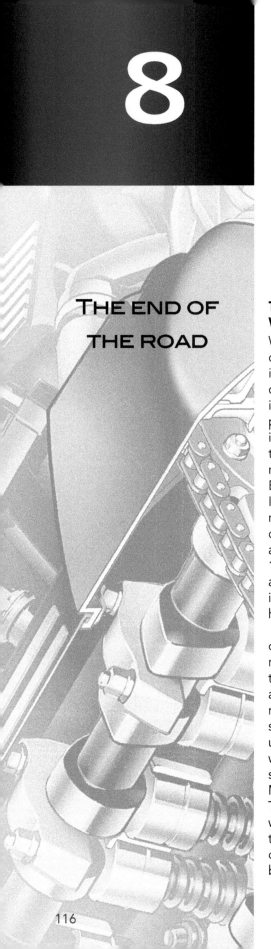

8

THE END OF THE ROAD

THE M535I RETURNS ... ALONG WITH THE NEW M5!

When it comes to moving cars off the showroom floor, the importance of image cannot be overstated. Carefully managed, it can cause mental autopilot in potential buyers, inducing an irresistible urge to spend now! By the mid to late eighties, there was no escaping the fact that the E12/E28 design 5 Series was ageing. In October 1986, *Motor's* factfile noted that "5 – BMW's old man of the range – the 5 Series – first appeared as far back as September 1972." BMW was busy working on an all-new successor, so, in the interim, the present model would have to carry on.

An image boost, a sprinkling of PR, never goes amiss. BMW released the M535i in the twilight of the E12's days to drum up interest, and the E28 was going to be the recipient of the same Dynasty-style shoulder pads treatment to stir up the customer base. The result was no fewer than three 3.5-litre specials for 1984/5: the 535i, the M535i and the all-conquering M5! The 535i and the M535i were E28s with firmed up suspension and, in the case of the latter, a full colour coded, multi-piece integrated bodykit.

Both cars featured the by now ubiquitous 218bhp 3430cc small bore, long stroke, 3.4-litre M30. As commented on by *Motor* late in 1984, the cars were to be constructed on the regular production line and sold in relatively large numbers. A British market BMW advert from 1985 stated that the 535i and M535i were separated by 550 pounds sterling and the latter's visually enhancing bodykit. Both versions were available with the BMW, ZF collaborated, four-speed, electro hydraulic ZF 4HP autobox.

When *Motor* informed British readers about the upcoming M535i, in an article entitled "M is for Mouthwatering," mention was made of how BMW's PR machine worked almost as well as its cars. The 535i and M535i both had 218bhp and 3.5 litres, Herr Bovensiepen's Alpina B9 package possessed 245bhp from his company's version of the same M30 motor. A natural question in light of such overmanning is what is the difference between the Alpina B9 and the M535i? BMW's response was brief and to the point "about 5000 pounds".

Testers noticed that the BMW M535i lacked the punch of the Alpina B9. Even so, the M535i was

The 245bhp Alpina B9, was the best known Alpina of its early to mid 1980s era. Only 64 RHD UK B9s were sold.
(Courtesy Peter Thorpe)

an extremely pleasant car, and it did cost a whole lot less than that rarefied B9! *Motor's* Peter Frater spent more than a little time buzzing along at 6000rpm in the close ratio Getrag's fifth cog on the German autobahn. This entailed a terminal velocity of 143mph, so the M535i wasn't short on squirt. The M535i proved a very impressive sight with its bonnet open whilst on display at the 1984 Paris Auto Salon!

Enough of the off-the-peg variety; what of the M5? The M5 was more along the lines of the custom 1979-1981 E12 M535i.

In other words, a largely hand constructed, Motorsport factory, manual gearbox only, low volume special. It was simply denoted M5, the first time such a designation was used. It lacked the M535i bodykit that *CAR* magazine thought had been mocked up by Boy Racers Inc.

There was nothing on the outside to alert casual observers to the race track derived 3453cc motor. This item was shared with the M635CSi, a star of the 1983 Frankfurt Motorshow. The 286bhp engine gave the M5 a top speed of over 150mph, a shade faster than

the heavier M635CSi. Sprinting to sixty from a standing start took at the very most 6.5 seconds. Where did the engine originate? The answer would have to be on the racetrack. It represented just about the ultimate incarnation of the Alex von Falkenhausen-led, 1968/9-launched M30 inline 6.

BMW had campaigned against Ford of West Germany for supremacy in the then European Touring Car Championship back in the early seventies. The rules were open to interpretation, the money was big and the results were explosive. Big technology, super

Alpina not only makes excellent automobiles, it also produces some fine wines! Sytner BMW, started by Frank Sytner, has been the Alpina agent in the UK for several years. (Courtesy Alpina GB)

high power outputs, and drivers tempted from Formula One, not to mention Formula One-wide rubber! These were the hallmarks of the expensive ETCC. Of course, it was even more expensive if you weren't winning, and BMW wasn't. In the game of automotive one-upmanship BMW was coming off second best to Ford. However, the small Bavarian firm had a cunning plan!

The first shot fired was a racegoing version of the 2.8-litre 2800CS, and the game largely ended in 1973 with a normally-aspirated 370bhp, 24-valve, 3.5-litre, short stroke, dry sump version of the M30 in a 1060 kilo version of the CS coupé. BMW triumphed over Ford in the final showdown. Different personnel and some timely exploitation of the rule book saw BMW reach the summit first. After that the ETCC deflated. The fuel crisis and spiralling championship costs meant that the zenith had been passed. No fear, BMW had made its point and, in the expensive arena of European motorsport, one does withdraw after a triumph.

The 3453cc motor had a big bore and short stroke, quite natural in racing where you want a motor that will stack on the revs quickly, and hold together at very high engine speeds. It continued to be campaigned in motorsport, in the BMW CS coupé. In 1978 it made a limited appearance in the exotic Giugiaro-styled, mid engined M1, complete with dry sump and racing style mechanical injection. The South African market 745i and European market M635CSi were the first sightings of the race derived engine in something approaching a regular BMW range member.

Once out of the M1 the 3453cc engine dumped the Kugelfischer Bosch mechanical injection, dry sump and 9 to 1 compression ratio. The M5 had 10.5 to 1 compression and Bosch DME, not a bad idea if you want to put a highly tuned engine in a road car and wish to maintain driveability. In spite of its discreet appearance the M5 was quite an image maker, able to cruise at 155mph one moment, and crawl along at a snail's pace with air-conditioning the next. It was the sort of practical performance

Unlike BMW's M cars, Alpinas kept
BMW's econogauge. This B9 has the
optional BMW factory a/c. The Alpina
B9 was good for an honest 145mph.
(Courtesy Peter Thorpe)

The famous 245 horse naturally
aspirated Alpina SOHC two-
valve 3.5-litre six. Gutsier than
BMW's 3.5-litre two-valver. Tuners
stuck to the two-valve M30.
(Courtesy Peter Thorpe)

Outside West Germany, importing agents like Sytner BMW created Alpinas by adding imported Alpina items to standard cars. The UK B9 used the 528i as a base car. (Courtesy Peter Thorpe)

Alpina loved its stripe decorations. Each Alpina's spec was decided by the individual customer. (Courtesy Peter Thorpe)

Pretty rare, but as this 1988 UK M5 shows, one could specify the M535i's M Technic bodykit on the street sleeper M5. (Courtesy Jamie Myles)

A genuine 286bhp M88 3.5-litre E28 M5 motor. The M5, and M535i, were E28 runout specials. To combat all the attention and sales, Stuttgart was getting with its MB 200-300 W124. (Courtesy Jamie Myles)

car more and more folks around the world wanted. When it reached the British market the M5 cost approximately 31,000 pounds sterling, or 10,000 pounds over the price of the relatively affordable M535i.

In what was now par for the course with BMW's European performance versions, the M5 featured TRX rims and rubber, and was set up to drink 98 octane leaded petrol. These are two problems to consider in owning an M5 of this

vintage today. The Michelin metric sized tyres are expensive and hard to source, and the M5's motor was designed for use with 98 octane leaded gas in mind. Also, the M88 motor needs more frequent and expensive maintenance, versus a

The stuff of childhood dreams indeed. However, 1986-88 was a tense time at BMW. The E28 was ageing, and Munich couldn't wait for the new E34 5 Series to arrive. (Courtesy Jamie Myles)

The M88 was used in the M635CSi, South African E23 745i, and E28 M5. It was the first time said powerplant had been used in wet sump form. This one has been tuned to 320bhp! (Courtesy Jamie Myles)

A conventional handbrake and manual gearbox! The overdrive Getrag 280/5 went well with the 3.73:1 final drive. M cars didn't have the tachometer-placed fuel economy gauge.

When first released, the E28 M5 used metric TRX rims, but, in the end, conventional 16-inch hoops and Pirelli rubber were substituted. (Courtesy Richard Stern)

normal M30 big six – all related to the DOHC, 24-valve layout.

The biggest surprise was BMW's decision to sell the E28 M5 in the States, in effect a federally sanctioned new car covered by a BMW warranty. Just the ticket to keep the gray market at bay and liven up the relatively mundane BMW US line-up. By selling it in the last year the E28 5 Series would be offered in the US, the M5 would raise public awareness of the 5 Series, the perfect lead-in to the US introduction of the E34 5 Series for the 1989 model year.

The US M5 was largely untainted by US Federal dictates, although, it did have the mandatory 5mph bumpers, plus modifications to allow it to drink unleaded fuel with a catalytic converter, knocking 30bhp off the European version's tally. Apart from this, and the somewhat limited colour choice, US buyers could very nearly sample the best that BMW had to offer.

The US M5 was available only as a 1988 model year car in black exterior paint. Originally only 500 US M5s were to be imported; in the final analysis, 1235 examples made it to US shores, resulting in some purchasers feeling short-changed vis-a-vis exclusivity and a bit miffed that they weren't going to make as much as they could have done at resale time. Some banded together to lodge a false advertising lawsuit. However, the less said about such speculator driven legal action, the better.

Nelson Piquet's 1983 F1 World Championship-winning Brabham BMW Turbo utilized a BMW M10 4 cyl production block. (Courtesy BMW)

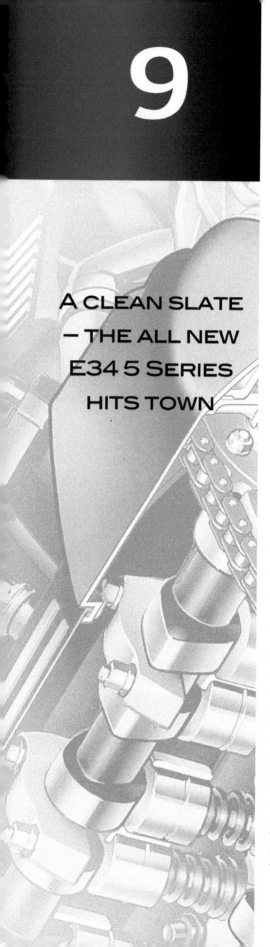

9

A CLEAN SLATE – THE ALL NEW E34 5 SERIES HITS TOWN

TURBULENT TIMES AT BMW 1982-85

1962 to 1982 marked a period of sustained success and achievement at BMW, a continuous stream of increasingly profitable model introductions unmatched in the auto industry before or since. With more than just a small degree of good fortune, BMW was able to combine winning sales figures with hard-to-achieve critical acclaim.

Inevitably, however, boom periods don't last, and the lead-up to the introduction of the third instalment of the 5 Series encountered some difficult hurdles. Whilst some of the problems were attributable to BMW's chosen path, most were beyond the company's control.

BMW's strong background in technology matters actually started to work against it. Between the mid 1970s and mid 1980s, much attention was directed at under-bonnet and dashboard electronics. While there is little doubt that advances brought genuine efficiency gains and bolstered sales, they were perhaps not as readily apparent as a jello mould body shape with flush fitting, noise reducing glass. More seriously, the great emphasis on all things electronic had left the door

open to the motor car's number one foe, the auto gremlin. There were teething problems with the fledgling electronic gizmos, and it's no secret that the original E23 7 Series had something of a reputation in West Germany for taking unscheduled autobahn naps!

There was some difficulty taming engine management problems when mating the two M60 baby sixes to create the prototype 4.5-litre V12 of the late 1970s. Microprocessor controlled woes were another reason a raft of technical aids were put on ice in the mid 1980s. In September 1985, Britain's *CAR* magazine mentioned the somewhat embarrassing result that the large bimmers had come last on the most recent German ADAC roadside recovery chart. The image of stranded owners on a motorway hard shoulder was not exactly in keeping with the hard fought reputation for dependability BMW had up to that point. The transition from having a computer governing air, fuel mixture to air, fuel and ignition timing, while invaluable for a future with lower octane fuel, was proving rougher than expected. These were the early days for Bosch Motronic, a time when such a system was

The entry level four-cylinder 518i, after a late 1990 start, was available by the time of the E34's demise. It's shown here in final 518i SE trim, with the M43 I4. (Courtesy Darren Kelly)

The E34's high tech image, was unsurpassed in 1988. It looked sharp, drove very well, and had Stuttgart's W124 scared! Metric TRX rims were early E34 fare. (Courtesy Goodyear)

In April 1988, *CAR* magazine declared that the E34 525i was a sports car masquerading as a saloon. It was a more than dynamic match for the Benz W124. (Courtesy Craig Reeves)

selectively introduced in single model variants. It wouldn't be long before having a computer govern air, fuel mix and ignition timing was the rule rather than the exception. The prospect of tighter emission laws and unleaded fuel loomed large even in Europe; Bosch Motronic would be an essential companion on the road in an increasingly strictly policed environment.

Noises were coming from certain quarters that BMW's research and development department was stagnating. In the early to mid 1980s there were a number of reshuffles in personnel. In 1983, Eberhard von Kuenheim fired R&D head Karlheinz Radermacher. The media put this decision down to Radermacher being too conservative. Hans Hagen stepped into the breach after coming from truck manufacturer MAN, and was himself replaced relatively quickly by contemporary BMW rising star Wolfgang Reitzle. The reshuffle didn't stop with people; the familiar faces comprising BMW's model range were due for a shake up.

BMW, a midget in a world dominated by auto giants, had spent up big on a new wave of models for the 1970s. This was a point not lost on Britain's magazine *Motor* when introducing the brand new original 7 Series back in 1977. It noted that BMW was having quite a decade, with no less than four model ranges introduced in the space of less than 5 years. The new 5, 3, 6 and 7 Series cars were largely an unqualified success: modern, refined and a friend to motoring journalists and buyers alike. However, the act of creating such accomplished world stage protagonists doesn't come cheap. Once the cars were released, BMW had to be content with small changes and carefully introduced refinements to allow a good initial design to pay for itself over a long production run.

Even excellent designs can grow stale, at least in the image conscious eyes of mainstream buyers, after years of exposure. Understandably, the fraternity of motoring jounalists greeted BMW's decision to launch lightly facelifted second drafts of the 5 and 3 Series, in 1981 and 1983 respectively, with the universal cry that too little had been done after too long. BMW

The E34 had that bold, upmarket look, perfectly suited to the 'Dynasty Decade' that was the power-dressing 1980s! A 525i SE is present. (Courtesy Craig Reeves)

As with the E28, spartan luxury and the angled dashboard were back. As ever, the stick shift was a sporty BMW drawcard. (Courtesy Craig Reeves)

The E34 5 Series was better packaged than previous Fives, but critics still thought rear seat space was a little tight. The cost of rear drive is space efficiency. (Courtesy Craig Reeves)

had little alternative, however, as development costs had to be amortised; the new wave of the '70s had to hold out for just a little longer. BMW was a small company, money was tight and the early '80s were turbulent times. BMW took the prudent move of releasing the redeveloped and reoriented E28 and E30 for the economy, technology conscious times of the early '80s. However, outside forces threatened to derail the BMW game plan.

In 1984 the metal workers of West Germany embarked on a costly strike activity to achieve a 35 hour working week. It was a drawn-out piece of industrial action that had negative ramifications for the German auto industry at home and overseas. The strike started on May 14th and BMW was forced to shut up shop just four days later. The real danger for BMW was the head start given to rivals in the increasingly important export markets whilst BMW was out of action due to the strike. BMW chairman Eberhard von Kuenheim stated at the time: "In the US we have already lost the '84 motorcycle business to the Japanese." Needless to say, American luxury car makers like Cadillac and Lincoln, plus upscale imported makes, were free to make the most of the US market, too.

BMW's chief headache in 1985

To stay competitive BMW switched in mid 1990 to 24-valve DOHC M50 sixes. The 525i was boosted from 170 to 192bhp. (Courtesy Craig Reeves)

Established in 1978 by racer Michael Krankenberg, by the mid 1990s MK-Motorsport catered to E31 8 series, E34 5 Series and E36 3 Series. MK-Motorsport is well known for its block pattern alloys. (Courtesy MK-Motorsport)

was confusion over future emission standards in the home West German market, and continental Europe as a whole. June 28th 1985 became something of an eleventh hour climax when the EEC reached a consensus over emission regulations for the period October 1989 to October 1993. Environmental groups in Germany wanted the fullscale US standards to protect their forests. What resulted was a compromise that gave a relieved car industry some concrete limits to work with for the future. The West German government had pushed hard for the blanket use of catalytic converter-equipped cars using tax concessions, this was thwarted by EEC Commissioners who severely reduced the number of concessions.

This was where BMW got into commercial trouble. The company took a gamble that the future of motoring in Europe would be the catalytic converter, petrol route. This is what had happened in the States and it seemed logical that Europe would follow a similar path. So BMW took the step of offering regular models in unleaded, three-way catalyst form for a mere 500 pounds sterling surcharge. The immediate result was that BMW captured 52% of the market for catalytic converter equipped cars. The downside of the strategy was that the market for unleaded catalyst cars turned out to be smaller than originally anticipated. BMW's sales for the first quarter of 1985 were only 31,967 units, a figure exceeded by the Daimler-Benz 190 alone! There was some light at the end of the tunnel, however, as home market buyers that had put off purchasing decisions until the dust had settled vis-a-vis the environment, returned

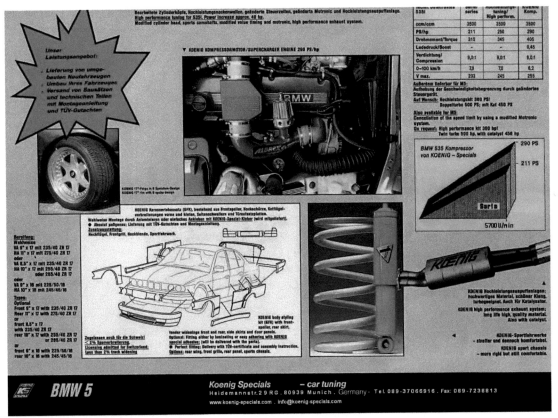

Willy Koenig's tuning firm had the hardware for the E34 5 Series. This included a twin turbo conversion for the M5 3.6, which yielded 500 horses! (Courtesy Koenig-Specials)

Koenig-Specials worked with E34 M30 535is, the E34 M5s, and offered supercharger kits for 540i/740i & 840i V8s. (Courtesy Koenig-Specials)

BMW's quad circular eyewear has become a familiar sight since the late '60s BMW six-cylinder saloons and coupés. However, since the E36 3 Series of the early '90s, new models have had the lamps placed behind clear plastic covers. (Courtesy Paul Baylis)

to the BMW fold. They flooded back to BMW, in fact, and helped achieve its second best sales quarter ever.

Apart from the temporary bleakness of 1974, BMW had managed to finish each financial year of recent times in the black. Even in 1985 it could honestly say that its factories were churning out at full capacity. But grey clouds were gathering on the home front: by September 1985 a huge 70% of BMW's production was going to overseas markets. This was quite an about-face for a company that didn't get into the export game for real until 1966!

CONTENDING WITH MERCEDES
BMW could pat itself on the back for achieving a strong foothold in Japan, and achieving greater success in the large US market, but this didn't alter the fact that things were looking shaky on the domestic scene by 1985. Critics were lining up to proclaim that BMW was ignoring the domestic market, and gleefully pointed out that, unlike BMW, Porsche and Daimler-Benz could charge over the odds prices both at home and overseas. There was no escaping the fact that BMW models carried

lower list prices than equivalent Daimler-Benz products. When you also consider that West German market bimmers were regularly discounted and generally available for immediate delivery, while there was a waiting list for every Mercedes model, and each easily made its list price, it becomes quite obvious that BMW was not having an easy time at home. For the price of an MB 500 SEC, the West German buyer could purchase a BMW M635CSi. Obviously, BMW was struggling to convince people that this was a bargain.

There had been a real change in public perception of the Stuttgart and Munich rivals. Daimler-Benz, for so very long the purveyor of staid family saloons for well-heeled grandpapas, was actually turning trendy! The '80s brought new wave models like the compact 190 and mid ranger W124 200/300 that, in short order, were perceived in Germany and around the world as technically superior, sportier and more fun to drive; quite a reversal of roles.

BMW had generated favourable publicity in Formula One racing by powering Nelson Piquet's 1983 world championship winning Brabham, so wasted little time in alerting potential buyers to the fact that the Formula One four pot turbo motor shared its block with contemporary 1.8-litre BMWs. After all, the Brabham Formula One engine was actually based on the old four-cylinder M10. Around the same time came the BMW M635CSi that made its first media foray at the 1983 Frankfurt Motorshow, a great image builder for BMW.

Success in racing and high profile road cars aside, BMW

couldn't get away from the fact that its mainstream models were ageing. There were no new models to cast before the public, BMW was a small car maker in a part of the model cycle where it had to be content with sitting out this dance.

In this respect, *CAR* magazine was correct to point out that the final two-and-a-half years for the then current E28 5 Series would be onerous. Slight technical and cosmetic revisions, and the arrival of the M535i/M5, were the automotive 'garnish' that allowed the current E28 to eke out its final days with a modicum of buyer interest. The new E34 5 Series was waiting in the wings, so all would be well again in bimmer land, right? Not quite, as even the design work on the E34 wasn't going as smoothly as planned. Some senior people at BMW felt that initial proposals were just too bland and similar to the current model. As the current model was generally considered too similar to the previous model, it was obvious that something had to be done, and fast! So it was that the E34 was reworked yet again along bolder lines. However, the tide of fortune was about to turn in BMW's favour.

BMW'S 1986 RENAISSANCE
BMW did some valuable reheating of its volume seller, the E30. The lack of a four-door variant had been the Achilles heel of the baby BM for quite some time. BMW handily plugged that model gap and followed this up with worthwhile revisions to the E30 for 1986 and 1988. The idea was to redeploy the E30 above the mainstream market segment where it was being eaten up by equipment, price conscious offerings from non prestige

manufacturers. The strategy worked, with more than a little assistance from the all-conquering touring car slayer known as the M3.

Quite remarkably the E30 achieved better sales figures in the second half of its life, the touch of image tonic had done the trick. BMW pulled off a similar glamour victory at the top end of town with the new 1987 E32 7 Series. For so long Daimler-Benz had been the market's top dog for ultra expensive luxo barges, but the new 7 Series turned the tables on the W126 S class. The E32 was bold, modern and an immediate success all over the world. After spending nearly 20 years in the sales shadow of Daimler-Benz, BMW released a leader that was dressed to kill. The crowning moment of BMW's late '80s mini revival was the launch of the all-new E34 5 Series.

When a car maker finds a successful style or formula that the public takes to its heart and readily associates with a marque, it can be very difficult to find new ground. Ferrari got into this very position with the Pininfarina 308 GTB and GTS cars of 1975. The 308 became the recognisable face of Ferrari and, when the model came up for replacement, stylists had a hard time finding the next step. The biggest worry is that even if the car maker has the guts to go a different way, the public still wants the flavour it's grown accustomed to, even whilst clamouring for something new and modern.

BMW was saddled with just such a corporate look. The life-saving 1500 of the early sixties brought styling and engineering traits that would stretch on at BMW into the late '80s. As far as looks went this implied a low belt line, tall greenhouse, boxy silhouette, and incorporation of the traditional BMW kidney grille for front end treatment. Apart from changing tastes, by the time the E34 came along there were dictates working against the BMW look. Designers had to factor in the better aerodynamic efficiency necessary for lower wind noise and better fuel consumption at the higher cruising speeds European buyers were expecting. Higher speeds on continental autoroutes required reduced front end lift and greater rear downforce.

With the 1968 XJ6, Jaguar was able to introduce a cutting edge saloon whilst retaining traditional identity, in spite of the complete absence of exterior identification insignia. Could BMW perform the same trick with the new 5? The answer would have to be an unreserved yes! The E32 7 Series and E34 5 Series marked a bold departure from the look associated with bimmerdom for the last quarter century, but still incorporated some visual elements from the recent past.

They passed the acid test of public approval. From the start buyers identified the new cars as BMWs and, like their predecessors, they were an instant commercial hit. Credit Claus Luthe for taking BMW into a new era of public approval. He had massaged the E12 into the E28 under specific instructions to be conservative. Now the gloves were off and the new cars were true to their goal of being a bold break with the past.

The new 5 wasn't just good for a BMW, it elevated BMW to the top of the executive car game in looks and ability. This was very much apparent when *CAR* procured an early pre-production 525i for one of its Giant Test stouches. The competition took the form of the trail-blazing jelly mould Audi 100 2.3E and current executive car champ Mercedes 230E. The fickle follower of fashion would have claimed that the Audi was out of date, appearance-wise. The tubular flanks, long front and rear overhangs, cigar shaped body and narrow track dated Ingolstadt's contender in its present company. While no one could say such a thing about the relatively new Daimler Benz W124, there was little doubt that it lacked the freshness of the newly released E34 5 Series. Daimler Benz's W124 could no longer launch merciless attacks on the ageing E28 5 Series, its honeymoon period had ended. There was a new kid on the block, a new leader of the pack, and it had just served notice!

E34 – A BIGGER 5 SERIES

On to a few vital statistics. The new 5 was 3.9 inches longer, 2 inches wider, had a wheelbase extended by some 5 inches and had marginally reduced ground clearance. It had a wider, lower, sleeker look that some 2002 aficionados might have had difficulty warming to. The E34 had an aggressive spin on the wedge shape theme. The long-wheelbase was combined with remarkably – remarkably for BMW, that is – truncated front and rear overhangs. Short front and rear overhangs were soon to become established BMW practice in the near future on cars like the 1992 E36 3 Series.

However, in the midst of so much change Claus Luthe was able to work in a few family favourites so that long-time BMW worshippers

The 525i SE was the perfect blend of economy, performance and luxury in Britain. By 1995, all E34s shared the V8's winged kidney grille. (Courtesy Ollie Juggins)

wouldn't feel neglected. That familiar C pillar was back for another tour of duty and, even though the roof section was a smidgen lower and with less glass than in years gone by, nobody could say that the E34 had joined the high waisted brigade just yet. In spite of the need to reduce the frontal area for lower drag, the familiar bimmer frontal treatment was incorporated. The kidney grille became even squatter and was now body coloured! Even so, it was still flanked by the virtually trademark, four equal sized headlamps. Without having to raid the retro parts bin, BMW had successfully entered a new age.

Style is one thing, but it needs something to back it up. The E34's clean slate allowed BMW to take matters to a new technical plateau. Worthy though the E12/E28 design was, there was room for improvement in the areas of aerodynamics, safety, driving dynamics and refinement. The new E34 had a fashionably low drag coefficient of between 0.30 and 0.32, depending on the version at hand. Ellipsoidal eyewear meant the designers could use smaller headlamps and shrink the car's frontal area. At the rear, BMW had the chance to introduce a raised rear deck that blended into the holistic style of the new car. The preceding E28 was also designed with a raised rear deck in the interest of increased downforce. However, this embellishment was somewhat at odds with the underlying Bracq-inspired E12 shape.

With the world price of petroleum distillate generally falling, the E34's thorough grounding in aerodynamics was intended to reduce cabin noise at speed as much as it was to improve fuel efficiency. A shape designed to cleave through the air with minimal resistance would have a greater chance of avoiding tiresome glass and pillar induced wind roar at higher cruising speeds. The new 5 would have terminal velocities of twenty or thirty miles per hour higher than envisaged for roadgoing versions of the old E12 back in the early seventies. So abandoning the typical BMW profile would allow bearable cruising above 120mph on the autobahn.

Unfortunately, the move to low drag exposed BMW to the problem many other low drag adherents experienced: airflow disturbed high speed stability. Throughout automotive history it has been accepted that low drag teardrop shapes are susceptible to being blown off course by crosswinds and the disturbed airflow generated by passing vehicles like lorries. This was the reason Ford of Europe came up with the bi-plane spoiler for the high-performance Sierra XR4i back in the early eighties. *CAR*'s April 1988 Giant Test involving the new 525i did record that the BMW didn't behave as erratically as the W124 Mercedes 230E, which often required one-and-a-half lanes of the motorway to stabilise itself. Hardly reassuring when travelling at speeds in excess of 100mph!

Primary and secondary safety often goes hand-in-hand with refinement, and the new E34 certainly had something worthwhile to offer in these two key areas. It could be said that the new 5 Series profited by sharing floorpan sections and suspension components with the physically larger E32 7 Series. In days gone by the 5 Series was a size smaller than the 7 Series and, whilst drivetrain components were a common factor, both were unrelated physically. Indeed, the E12 and E28 5 Series were closely

You could have wood, heated leather seats, and more, but BMW still didn't have the luxury feel of a Caddy or a Jag. Call it spartan luxury! (Courtesy Ollie Juggins)

At 185.8in long, the E34 was a much bigger 5 Series, similar to the E23 7 Series in overall size and weight.
(Courtesy Ollie Juggins)

By 1993, BMW had brought variable valve timing (Single Vanos) to its 2/2.5-litre sixes. The power remained the same, but the delivery was more even. (Courtesy Ollie Juggins)

Taillights were in the E32 7 Series 'L-style,' and indeed, at first glance the E34 was hard to tell apart from its big brother. (Courtesy Ollie Juggins)

related to the 6 series with which it shared a chassis, at a time when little was said about such matters. The new 5 was moving up a size and Computer Aided Design was utilised to improve upon previous iterations of BMW's medium sized unibody. Measurements in the static state showed the newcomer to possess 43% greater flexural and 70% higher torsional rigidity. In the dynamic state both areas showed a 30% improvement.

The E34 was designed to cope with frontal impacts of up to 35mph whilst keeping the body's survival cell intact. At the time, US Federal crash testing dictated that a vehicle be able to withstand impacts into a fixed barrier at 30mph. Whilst the 5mph buffer may not sound very much, it implied that the E34's structure could deal with an extra 35% of energy being absorbed by its steel structure. While targets have been raised since the late eighties, it says something for BMW that many contemporary designs came off worse in independent testing above the then mandatory 30mph requirement.

Britain's *What Car?* reported on just such an independent test conducted by the German TÜV vehicle testing organisation and the University of Heidelberg's institute for Legal Medicine and Injury Research. The 520i E34 used in the test out-performed the Mercedes W124 and Volvo 740 in the standardised 34mph offset crash test. Concrete proof that BMW's unseen R&D work had paid off in this important area. It was also surprising to see how poorly contemporary designs, apart from those mentioned in the foregoing, performed when subjected to coping with the extra load energy.

The very qualities that endowed the E34 with good safety also gave superior driving characteristics that all enthusiasts want. A stronger, unflappable body structure means that the driver receives only the messages he wants and needs to hear. For the 5 Series driver

The new E34 5 Series, one of the more memorable 1988 new model releases. (Courtesy BMW)

this meant improved steering feedback and better wheel control over imperfect road surfaces when compared to the outgoing E28. What you didn't get was the unwelcome trio of noise, vibration and harshness that a staunch body structure magically filters out.

In *Fast Lane* Peter Dron wrote that the inward flexing of the MacPherson struts under heavy braking which bothered the E28 was unlikely to feature on the new E34 5 Series. On the subject of strength, the E34's bumpers could not be ignored. The new bumpers, or a combination of impact boxes and hydraulic dampers, to be more precise, were designed to cope with shunts of up to 9mph with reduced repair costs and no damage to engine mounts. BMW was putting the lessons learnt with impact bumpers on the seventies US market cars into wider practice. The new 5 Series bumpers could take everything the old impact bumpers could without ruining the car's overall shape.

The other benefit of having a car that doesn't mind being thrown headlong into concrete blocks is improved refinement. If one had to sum up the various 5s in single words the E12 would be sporty, the E28 technical and the E34 simply refined. The E34 was also sporty and technically accomplished, of course, but its development and execution were especially directed toward achieving exemplary refinement. Indeed, this aspect marks something of a watershed in the evolution of the 5 Series. From 1988, 5 Series models had noticeably different characters.

The new 5 shared body hardware with the E32 7 Series, which was itself physically larger and heavier than its E23 predecessor. Extensive use of sound-deadening material was made on the E34 5 Series, adding over 110lb in weight per car; pure extravagance at the height of the 1974 fuel crisis, this was now strangely acceptable, and, given changing buyer tastes, even

Whether it was the 150bhp or 2-litre displacement, the 520i was a fiscal limit for road tax, insurance or company car tax allowance in Europe. (Courtesy Mario Papakyriacou)

necessary. Apart from the obvious sound dungeon of the engine bay, sound-deadening material was even placed in the E34's A and C pillars and rubber mats resided under the rear bench seat.

In place of the coarse, short hair, bauble like carpet that adorned the floor of the E12 was thickly padded, rich, plush carpet, and even the headlining of the E34 was composed of noise absorbent

The E34's success wasn't hidden under a bushel. The new Five was putting the heat on Mercedes' W124 and Audi's 100. (Courtesy Mehrdad Zarifkar)

All E34s carry over 100lb of sound absorbing material, including foam-filled A and B pillars, making even the powerful M5 sound suitably subdued. (Courtesy Mike Wong)

In view of the prodigious firepower some versions have, it's just as well that BMW gave the E34 a more neutral chassis than previous fives. Even with the powerful M5, the transition to oversteer was now quite gradual. (Courtesy Mike Wong)

material. Hydraulic engine mounts and special driveline bushings also played incremental roles in bringing hush to the E34's interior. The new 5's interior was library-quiet when compared to earlier incarnations, and, as with TV commercials for household detergents, there were gentlemen in white lab coats with clipboards ready to supply the fine details. Looking at independent sources there is proof that BMW had turned out a comparative mobile sound booth on wheels.

When *C&D* tested a US 530i in 1975 no less than 84 decibels were registered in the interior under full throttle acceleration; for the uninformed that's quite some din! Embarrasingly, the same reading was recorded for the same test *C&D* carried out on the 7.5-litre 1973 Pontiac Firebird Trans Am SD 455. 84 decibels may have been acceptable for a rip-roaring pony car from hell, but was not good news for a luxury saloon with a high price.

For the record, the initial E34 535i exposed its occupants to no greater than 75 decibels, even under the most trying of circumstances, an improvement that really could be noticed. The upshot of all these R&D travails was that the new 5 was an even better mile muncher than its predecessors. Georg Kacher, when writing for *Automobile Magazine*, mentioned that information rather than irritations reached the pilot. Peter Albrecht noted in *Sports Car*

Illustrated that the autobox 535i on test simply loped along the US interstate at speeds in excess of 120mph.

The new E34 matched the E28 5 Series and E32 7s, with a traditional chassis layout. Despite the bold exterior and onboard gadgetry, the E34 still employed the double pivot MacPherson struts up front and the Trac-Link tempered, semi-trailing arm rear end utilised by the old E28. This was basically the same setup BMW had stuck with since the successful 1500 of 1961/2 launched BMW's second life. However, by now the talk of the town revolved around multi-link rear ends, and semi-trailing arms in any form were out of date, right? The Mercedes 190 had impressed many with its neutral ways, and it was particularly in vogue with tyre companies. It was an excellent blank canvas upon which to evaluate different tyre prototypes.

BMW was not resting on its laurels, and there were important changes for the third course in the 5 Series banquet. The front axle was positioned further forward with a heftier transverse bar placed behind. At the back the semi-trailing arms were more stiffly braced and had redesigned mounting points. Perhaps of greater import was the E34's 50/50 weight distribution, aided by putting the battery under the rear bench for the first time in 5 Series history. For years BMW had wrestled to curb the tendencies of its nose-heavy cars; it's no help in maintaining traction, and the reason why so many motoring scribes suggested placing a sack of potatoes in the boot to get the best from older 3 Series cars.

ASC, EDC & SERVOTRONIC

With the new wave E32 and E34 cars, BMW was about to cure the old twitchiness at the limit that had called for so much driver expertise in times gone by. While the old hardware was still in residence, the sudden oversteer of yore had been evicted for good. *CAR's* initial gander at the new 525i saw it mention that the new car was secure from snail's pace to high cornering speeds. When the limit was approached the driver was

After having a nose-heavy reputation for many years, the E34 brought near 50/50 weight distribution to the 5 Series for the first time. (Courtesy Quentin Pinner)

The rear drive 5 Series has never had the greatest internal packaging or space efficiency, but it's something that has only bothered motoring journalists. (Courtesy Quentin Pinner)

given full warning and a gentle breakaway ensued. At last, I hear you cry, a foolproof chassis that shuns the almost universal adherence to understeer at the limit.

For all the control freaks out there BMW was finally able to

Given the impact bumper sharing, it was tough to tell the US E34 from the Euro E34. A 1992 535i five-speed is shown. (Courtesy Mike Cekalovich)

introduce ASC and EDC. Delayed due to technical hiccups earlier in the eighties, these two electronic sentries were ready for the E34's European introduction in 1988/89. US customers had to wait, but, then again, for the last 15 years they had grown used to being the last to receive BMW's new tricks. This time around it wasn't Federal or EPA dictates that slowed their introduction but the need to get such devices working 100% before release in such a litigious market. The spectre of all those reported Audi 100s that

spontaneously accelerated was still fresh in people's minds, so nobody was going to risk any electronic oversights depleting market share after that debacle. BMW played it safe and went for the delayed introduction.

ASC, or automatic stability control, was BMW's first stab at traction control, commonplace today on even the most humble of cars, but something special in the late eighties. Wheelspin was electronically sensed and followed by a backing off of engine power until the situation was brought

under control. EDC, or electronic damping control, developed in association with Fichtel and Sachs, involved electronically manipulated adjustable shock absorber settings for optimum ride and handling.

The final new member in the electronic Holy Trinity was Servotronic speed sensitive, power assisted steering. Up to this point the world had grown used to power assistance that concentrated aid to tiller toils up to 5mph and used engine rpm as the chief variable. With Servotronic the power assistance was progressively

141

1992 was the final year for the two-valve, 3.5-litre straight six. During 1987-1992, BMW supplied this motor in one world spec 211bhp, unleaded 9:1 CR form. (Courtesy Mike Cekalovich)

backed off up to 65mph and the key ingredient was vehicular road speed.

Servotronic was an excellent idea in theory, but it had its detractors. The general consensus from the world's motoring press was that the steering was just too light, even when the magic 65mph barrier had been crossed. It was a difficult extra cost option to warm to, especially given that the E34's regular power steering was already quite excellent. The E34 was also the first 5 Series to dump the old throttle cable. The old linkage was being superceded by an electronic link to the engine management computer, one step closer to the day when we would all be flying by wire.

On the inside the BMW driver cockpit had been suitably revised for fashion and ergonomic gain. It was the same story of high quality, low key building blocks deployed in a functional form to aid the driver. The much copied driver angled dashboard was very much in evidence, along with some subtle changes. The once very upright instrument binnacle was blended into the profile of a gently sweeping contour, no real surprise as it was only reflecting the E34's integrated philosophy.

The E34 5 Series also heralded the return of that long-lost friend of the executive car, wood. It was consciously turfed on the E28, but with the E34 it would eventually become the permanent fixture it was on the old E12. Whether it was the bubinga wood from Africa or the later walnut seen on V8 5 Series

It was hard to find a manual five-speed BMW 535i/735i. Only 56 US 535is were so equipped. Stick shift 735is were rarer still. Dingolfing and BMW SA E34 production totalled 1,333,412 5 Series. (Courtesy Mike Cekalovich)

cars, wood was making a comeback and this time it was glossy! Gone was the once traditional restrained German dull silk finish: customers wanted high gloss. Now you could comb hair or touch up make-up without using the vanity mirror. In fact, the planks used on the post 1994 E class Mercedes were so shiny that some mistook them for plastic! The times they were a-changing. The inclusion of BMW's established dashboard toys, the check control panel and trip computer, pitching in with 18 and 12 functions respectively, were quite a contrast to the otherwise friends-of-the-forest look.

On to the more serious subject of heating, ventilation and air-conditioning, or HVAC. Time moves on and buyers, especially in warmer export markets, expect more with each passing year. The E34 represented BMW's first all-new medium size body structure since the 1972 520/520i. *R&T* once noted that the dashboard on the late sixties BMW six-cylinder saloons and coupés simply didn't permit a large enough evaporator/blower box for effective cooling in hot weather. In fact, the US journal mentioned it was something of a paradox that the air-conditioning in such an expensive saloon

couldn't match the performance of the unit in a humble contemporary family Chevrolet. The magazine concluded that every car has a downside and it was just something the BMW owner had to get used to. That comment was made in the early seventies and every year that followed BMW made worthwhile improvements.

For the first time the 5 Series had the same dashboard for air con and non-air con versions. There would no longer be the gaping hole in front of the shifter in non-air con versions. In Britain a/c was, at £955, an expensive

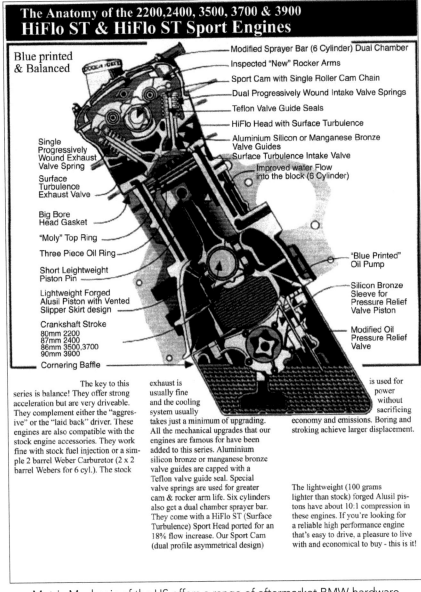

The Anatomy of the 2200, 2400, 3500, 3700 & 3900
HiFlo ST & HiFlo ST Sport Engines

Blue printed & Balanced

Modified Sprayer Bar (6 Cylinder) Dual Chamber
Inspected "New" Rocker Arms
Sport Cam with Single Roller Cam Chain
Dual Progressively Wound Intake Valve Springs
Teflon Valve Guide Seals
HiFlo Head with Surface Turbulence
Aluminium Silicon or Manganese Bronze Valve Guides
Surface Turbulence Intake Valve
Improved water Flow into the block (6 Cylinder)

Single Progressively Wound Exhaust Valve Spring
Surface Turbulence Exhaust Valve
Big Bore Head Gasket
"Moly" Top Ring
Three Piece Oil Ring
Short Leightweight Piston Pin
Lightweight Forged Alusil Piston with Vented Slipper Skirt design
Crankshaft Stroke
80mm 2200
87mm 2400
86mm 3500,3700
90mm 3900
Cornering Baffle

"Blue Printed" Oil Pump
Silicon Bronze Sleeve for Pressure Relief Valve Piston
Modified Oil Pressure Relief Valve

The key to this series is balance! They offer strong acceleration but are very driveable. They complement either the "aggressive" or the "laid back" driver. These engines are also compatible with the stock engine accessories. They work fine with stock fuel injection or a simple 2 barrel Weber Carburetor (2 x 2 barrel Webers for 6 cyl.). The stock exhaust is usually fine and the cooling system usually takes just a minimum of upgrading. All the mechanical upgrades that our engines are famous for have been added to this series. Aluminium silicon bronze or manganese bronze valve guides are capped with a Teflon valve guide seal. Special valve springs are used for greater cam & rocker arm life. Six cylinders also get a dual chamber sprayer bar. They come with a HiFlo ST (Surface Turbulence) Sport Head ported for an 18% flow increase. Our Sport Cam (dual profile asymmetrical design) is used for power without sacrificing economy and emissions. Boring and stroking achieve larger displacement.

The lightweight (100 grams lighter than stock) forged Alusil pistons have about 10:1 compression in these engines. If you're looking for a reliable high performance engine that's easy to drive, a pleasure to live with and economical to buy - this is it!

Metric Mechanic of the US offers a range of aftermarket BMW hardware, including bored and stroked M10 and M30 engines. The two-valve per cylinder, 3.9-litre I6 is rated at 300bhp net. (Courtesy Metric Mechanic)

and rarely seen option in Europe. It wasn't even standard on the M5 3.6, outside America. In America, a/c was standard on that market's two initial E34s: the 525i and 535i.

The physically bigger E34 and its larger nose section and underdash environs also helped by allowing larger hardware to be fitted, not to mention an air con and heater outlet between the rear seats and twin temperature controls for each half of the interior. The E28 had bucked the European trend of having rotary dials for heating and ventilation; the E34 BMW went back to the E12 style of having three rotary dials.

BMW also finally capitulated with regard to electric seat controls. Stuttgart rival, Daimler-Benz, had solved the problem of dealing with power seats that can be moved in several directions. For the W126 S Class of the eighties a miniature control in the shape of an actual seat did the bidding of both driver and front passenger. BMW chose to have several buttons placed on the handbrake console between the seats. Having all those buttons can get really confusing, so for the E34 BMW swallowed its pride and designed its own little voodoo seat controller for in-car occult ceremonies.

Regarding minutiae everything on the E34 was electric and heated! Apart from power seats, the use of heating elements extended to the reversing mirrors, windscreen washer nozzles and door locks. Even the interior reversing mirror had an electric servo servant that dipped the reflective pane when reverse was engaged. Let's also not forget the front seat arm rest, reverse rear seatbelts and boot mounted CD changer. Nobody could accuse the latest 5 Series of lacking the equipment demanded by buyers of the late eighties and early nineties, even if they were often extra cost options for European buyers.

Now that the introductory details of the E34 have been well met, what did the new model line-up look like? For the third and final time BMW would be calling on its small six, big six and lonely four. Initially, the European model list started with the 520i and 525i, both utilising revised versions of the M60 baby six. They complemented the larger capacity 530i and 535i. The E34

535i represented the dying days of BMW's use of the old M30 big six in mainstream models. While the excellent 2.4-litre turbo diesel six was immediately carried over, fans of the economy orientated 518i had to wait.

The 530i replaced the long-running 528i, and the 535i used the increasingly common 3.4-litre version of the M30 for the range topper. In the past BMW had spiced up the 5 Series line-up with the occasional sprinkling of a 3.5-litre variant, often with racing overtones. This time round the 535i was a regular member of the 5 Series clan. Changing market tastes, combined with the fact that the new 5 was heftier, made using larger displacement units a necessity. Detail fiends please note that the E34 525i used the small block six taken from the snappy E30 325i, rather than the smallest version of the M30 as had been done in years gone by. The 530i's engine was a larger displacement edition of the BMW baby six, while the 525e's 2.7-litre motor was no more. BMW's small six was an ace up Munich's sleeve, one which Stuttgart didn't have. It did sterling service in the E30 3 Series and E34 5 Series, whilst being half the double act that made up the

If one had the funds, AC Schnitzer could supply a bespoke shooting brake version of BMW's E34 Touring. A perfect blend of performance and practicality! (Courtesy AC Schnitzer)

The AC Schnitzer ACS5 represented the power of dreams. The firm's 3.7-litre M30 I6 produced 262bhp DIN – two more than Alpina's B10 3.5 six. (Courtesy AC Schnitzer)

5-litre V12 motor in the 750i/iL E32 7 Series Flagschiff.

If the E28 epitomised the era of universal adoption of fuel-injection, then the E34 marked the mass use of Bosch Digital Motor Electronics, or DME. L-jetronic entailed the engine management computer just keeping an eye on the air/fuel mix. In the interests of greater efficiency and reduced maintenance, the sphere of influence was extended to ignition timing. Unleaded fuel would soon become just as common in Europe as in the US, so having finer control and avoiding detonation was important, especially given how everything in the technical world is always on the margin.

Lead not only protected soft valve seats but was also the fuel's built-in octane booster. It's worth mentioning that British BMW adverts from around 1988 noted that British market leaded Motorsport cars could not switch to unleaded fuel. These cars were very much the exception, as BMW was gearing up for a Katalyser Motronic equipped range. Apart from the Motorsport exceptions, the entire BMW petrol line-up for 1988 had Motronic and could run happily on unleaded: every car from the humble new M40 powered 316i to the M70 motivated 750iL. Production of Bosch Motronic hardware had reached sufficient scale to reduce unit costs and most of the bugs were ironed out, too. The time was ripe for full-scale change.

BMW and other European car makers were meeting the letter of the law, but motor testers and buyers were not always pleased with the results. In the late eighties, many in Europe became acquainted with the detoxed motor. Those finalised EEC environmental laws implied that motors would be set up for the new continental norm of unleaded fuel and three-way catalytic converters. The new specification engines felt uninspired; they didn't rev as willingly, and coaxing them through the final part of the rev band was painful. In short, it was the same phenomenon US testers and buyers encountered back in the seventies when clean air became paramount to their legislators.

The situation was of particular concern to European motorists because their cars lacked the stacks of displacement that could suck up efficiency losses brought about by the new state of engine tune. British testers didn't like the new 2-litre, German market, 16-valve injected four pot that VW was putting into its performance models. Their preference lay with the British market, four star leaded, 1.8-litre version of the same powerplant. Some testers had the foresight to say that everyone in Britain had better get used to the new flavour because soon everything would taste like this! Similarly, BMW's respected 3.5-litre motor went through a 7 horsepower drop to 211bhp as part of the preparations for the European launch of 1987 models. Retarded ignition timing, unleaded fuel, the retrofit possibility of a catalytic converter, all implied the loss of pin sharp throttle response and refinement from familiar engines.

The M60 that powered the new 525i fell in the same boat. The 525i turned in great ultimate performance figures, but testers said the detoxed 170bhp motor lacked torque and response low down. BMW was working on new engines, and major revisions to existing ones, to get back on track with the changed order. There was the replacement of the 1.8-litre M10 of 1961/2 vintage with the all-new M40 four-cylinder units, at least as far as mainstream models were concerned. Senior driveline engineer Karlheinz Lange was behind the new 1.6 and 1.8-litre fours. They were lighter, more compact, thermodynamically more efficient, and had the valuable addition of knock control sensors. The last item would be invaluable in staving off detonation induced by a lower octane diet of unleaded fuel. The M40, and the subsequent revised M43, were seen in 1.8-litre form in the new 1990 E34 518i.

The 518i was quite a surprise package. It was a balanced, economical, entry level choice for value seeking buyers. It wasn't a marketing creation trying to cash in on more glamorous upmarket versions. *Autocar & Motor* tested both the two valves per cylinder 520i and the new 518i, and came out on the side of the four-cylinder car. In-gear acceleration was better in the M40-powered car, and there was a tangible superiority in engine response. The then current 520i motor wasn't in the chase. Europe's new detoxed scenario put greater emphasis on an engine's ability to breathe and digest lower grade unleaded fuel. BMW had created the new M40 with such constraints in mind and was about to do the same for its two-valve per cylinder baby sixes.

THE M50 24-VALVE BABY SIXES

The M60, more in terms of the 2.0 than the 2.5-litre, was not doing

AC Schnitzer's own 17in rims, Silhouette bodykit/pack with 30mm lowering job, plus adjustable 26mm front 19mm rear swaybars, all supplied the substance to complement the form. (Courtesy AC Schnitzer)

good business in the bulkier E34. Adding insult to injury, the M40 in the 318i was even showing up the 2-litre M60 in the 320i. The small six was ready for its biggest shake-up so far. BMW reworked its miniature king of refinement for the hard years ahead – the M60 would become the M50. The 2.0 and 2.5-litre M50 possessed four valves per pot and twin cams, but that's not all they had! Stereo cam motors take up more space, make more noise and weigh more than their mono cam brothers. BMW was up to more than just adjusting the specification sheet.

BMWs since the 1500 had a very low bonnet line. For this reason BMW typically canted its inline motors thirty degrees from the vertical to clear the steeply raked bonnet. The taller twin-cam would have to be canted an extra three degrees. To curb additional weight and noise, BMW used plastic, and I don't mean our flexible friend, the credit card! Plastic came in the form of a new intake manifold and camshaft cover noise dampener. The new thermo plastic breathing straw carried half the pounds when compared to its usual aluminium counterpart.

Apart from weight loss the more precise cross sections and lengths offered by the new apparatus facilitated better breathing, definitely nothing to sniff at. When it came to reducing the noise generated by the duplicated valve gear, BMW resorted to a

bogus camshaft cover. A fake plastic ribbed cover sat over the real McCoy to muffle any extra mechanical thrashing. An excellent audio result but less pleasing on the visual front. While the new engine was tilted 33 degrees from the vertical, the extra cover was still positioned 30 degrees from straight up. Underbonnet sights were slightly odd.

Bosch DME 3.1 played no small role in keeping the mechanical symphony playing in time. The new engines used sky high compression ratios – 10.5-to-1 for the 2.0 and 10-to-1 for the 2.5-litre – for better performance and economy, with the added constraint of using 95 octane unleaded. Knock sensors and sophisticated engine management hardware and software would be essential in keeping the train on the rails. The new four valves per cylinder arrangement increased the valve cross section area by 40% compared to the old 12-valve head. This brought an increase in airflow of between 30 and 59%; just ask the guy over there wearing the white lab coat!

The new small sixes also had one ignition coil per cylinder, a concept pioneered by the quirky Swedes at Saab. Plus new sparkplugs with a triangular outer electrode on three legs produced a hotter spark and double the standard plug life. In spite of the profusion of new age thinking in evidence, BMW was not

Continued complaints that the small sixes had uneven power delivery led to the development of the Vanos edition, which had variable valve timing on the intake side to strike a better balance between low speed torque and top end power. (Courtesy Dick Schneiders)

"...looks great value new and will always achieve high prices at any age."

"WHAT CAR?"

THIS CAR.

The BMW 518i has the lowest depreciation rate of any car in its class.

Indeed, after 30,000 miles,* an Audi 100 2.0E will lose twice as much on average. A Granada 2.0i LX, more than that.

Whilst a Rover 820i will show a depreciation rate over two and a half times as great.

But then, the BMW 518i is not only built to be first in engineering standards, it's also built to last.

Small wonder it's got the highest appreciation rating with the press.

To: BMW Information Service, Winterhill, Milton Keynes MK6 1HQ. Telephone 0908 249189
Please send me further information on the BMW 5 Series and the name of my local dealer.

(Mr, Mrs, Miss etc.)   Initial   Surname   211 AM 12.2

Address

Town/County   Post Code

Telephone   Present Car   Year of reg.

Age if under 18   **THE ULTIMATE DRIVING MACHINE**

BMW 518i SHOWN COSTS £17,165. PRICE INCLUDES. CAR TAX AND VAT BUT EXCLUDES ROAD FUND LICENCE AND AT AN ESTIMATED COST OF £420. BMW EMERGENCY SERVICE, DELIVERY AND NUMBER PLATES. DEPRECIATION FIGURES BASED UPON 1990 'G' REGISTRATION MODELS AT 30,000 MILES. SOURCE: CAP DEALDATA SYSTEM (RETAIL PRICES) JANUARY 1992. PRICES CORRECT AT TIME OF GOING TO PRESS. FOR TAX-FREE SALES PHONE 071 409 3355.

In November 1991, *What Car*'s Ralph Morton found the E34 518i to be a competent entry level executive car. Plus, quite good value. (Courtesy BMW)

about to upset the entire apple cart in one hit. The M50 still adhered to a thin wall cast iron block and marked BMW's return to the chain-driven camshaft. The 1977 M60 saw the use of a rubber belt at a time when BMW's established M10 and M30 both used chains. Rubber belts, as used by fifties technical innovator Hans Glas, promised greater refinement throughout the rev range.

In releasing its brand new, four-cylinder M40, BMW decided to use a two-valve, single cam version for the majority of models, and reserve the spicier, 16-valve version for the sportier 'S' variants. The marginally more frenetic 16-valver would be more at home in the sportier guises of the E30 318is, the two-valve versions were perfectly adequate for the mainstream 316i and 318i. Motoring critics and buyers gave the thumbs up to BMW's decision. Both the 316i and 318i were praised for their excellent performance and economy in the four-cylinder class. Everyone agreed that the new fours gave a much needed lift to BMW's base models. The old M10's work was done, the M40 would take up the baton from this point on.

This was about the same time that Ford of Europe replaced its pinto unit with the more modern zetec. Both the BMW M40 and Ford zetec were being hailed in Europe as the best four pots.

BMW's decision to stick with two-valve motors was further vindicated when German journal *60 Minutes* lined up the new Audi A4 against the Mercedes C180 and BMW 318i in 1994. Ultra conservative Daimler-Benz had joined the four-valve fraternity, Ingolstadt had reaffirmed its vorsprung durch technik philosophy by going for no

less than five valves, BMW – with the oldest car on test – stuck with two valves per pot. The test result gave BMW a first in the motor department. Gotz Leyrer noted that it was a sobering thought for the believer in technology that BMW's seemingly dated two-valve motor could match the exotic powerplants of its rivals whilst bettering their fuel economy. For the versatile saloon class BMW knew its approach delivered the right balance. While the M40 had Bosch Motronic and knock sensors, BMW eschewed the exotic cylinder head layout without penalty, lending credence to the old adage of choosing horses for courses!

So it was that the new M50 in the 5 Series married new features such as sequential fuel-injection to the established practice of cast iron blocks and chain drives. After all the targets of superior performance and better breathing for an emissions-conscious Europe had been met, did it really matter if some misguided soul glanced at the spec sheet and tutted when he saw that the M50 still had an iron block?

The new 2.0 and 2.5-litre motors produced 150 and 192bhp respectively, as opposed to their older counterparts' best efforts of 129 and 170bhp. Fuel economy remained static, but, given there was no problem in this area, there was no reason why it should have changed. The new motors had to rev more freely and deliver greater punch and they managed to score on both counts. They felt wide awake and, to take advantage of their increased power delivery and better breathing on the high end of the scale, the red line was raised to 6500rpm. They hit their marks with the added bonus of not needing

variable length intake runners, and a weight penalty of only 12 kilos.

But these are not fire-breathing Motorsport mile munchers, I hear you cry, why all the emphasis? Whilst the 520i and 525i may lack the sexy image of the M5, or even the 535i, one cannot deny their commercial importance. Even before the M50 arrived on the scene the 1989 sales figures showed that the little brothers contributed no less than 76% to E34 sales. In gasoline price-conscious Europe, manual transmission 520i and 525i cars carried considerable weight, metaphorically speaking!

It would have been a serious error to have an uncompetitive engine in this key market segment. Concentrating solely on high echelon versions destined for the US would have been akin to telling the majority of buyers that if they could not find bread perhaps they should eat cake! At first both 12 and 24-valve versions sold alongside each other with the more powerful M50 variants scaling at a mere DM 1200 premium. It didn't last long, though, as soon the 12-valvers were laid to rest permanently. Indeed, the 192bhp, 24-valve, 2.5-litre unit was so accomplished and versatile that it saw off the M30 powered, 188bhp, six-cylinder 530i in the British market. Hooked up to a stick shift, as was usually the case, the new 2.5 super hero could leap tall buildings in a single bound in both 3 and 5 Series.

Matters did not rest there, as the M50 was revised once again for 1993. Persistent criticism about the pokey power delivery of the small six led to BMW launching the Vanos version of the 2.0 and 2.5-litre powerplants. BMW had resorted to variable valve timing to give the miniature sixes some balance in their spread of power. It involved 2 sets of camshaft lobes, a mild set for low rpm trawling and a wild group for high rpm shots. Two engines in one? Well, not quite, but a definite improvement on the current versions. Somehow, BMW had trouble shaking the frantic signature that seemed ingrained in the small six.

Just for the record, BMW's Adolf Fischer, a major force behind the 2002 Turbo, gave the 2.3-litre in the 1978 323i its Jekyll and Hyde character. With the Vanos variant it seemed that the last traces of monster had been filtered out.

If you want to know what Vanos stands for, know that the Germans like to stack adjectives together and a literal translation into English wouldn't quite work out! Know also that you can tell a motor with the Vanos enhancement from one without by looking at the front of the motor. The Vanos editions have a bulge at the front of the cylinder head. Now you can't be hoodwinked by plaid wearing, tyre slapping car salesmen. No need to thank me.

The initial E34 5 Series line-up was exclusively straight six petrol powered! (Courtesy BMW)

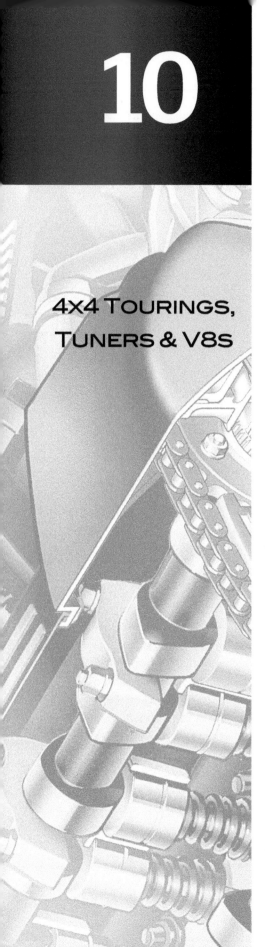

10

4X4 TOURINGS, TUNERS & V8S

THE E34 TOURING

Having the right stuff on hand is the subject of this chapter. BMW's major revival was based on identifying a market spot for a sporty, refined family saloon, above regular German Fords and Opels, but below more expensive and staid offerings from Daimler-Benz.

Unfortunately, the market is always in a state of flux, and a company wanting to stay ahead must look at what customers want at any given moment. BMW's experiences in the fifties showed that it simply wasn't enough to have well turned out models that people dreamed about. While Elvis Presley and John Surtees might have 507s, it didn't change the fact that BMW's glamorous range didn't pay for itself. The average person in the street couldn't afford a V8 BMW, and those who could didn't buy enough to cancel out the production costs. For BMW it was a case of technically good but no cigar.

For the nineties BMW brought out new versions, or introduced major revisions to existing models, with an eye to meeting changing tastes and opportunities. So would anyone like a 5 Series estate? While the idea of mixing the sport saloon gene pool with sprinklings of family hauler may seem odd, there was method in this madness.

Delve deeply into your memory vaults and you may recall the early seventies BMW Touring. It was a relatively short-lived, Michelloti-styled, three-door hatch based on the popular 02 series. It wasn't a big seller; that honour fell to the regular shoebox-shaped 02 saloon, and, as BMW's Hans Hagen told *CAR*, it was dropped before hot hatches became big news. Combine this with the fact that the restricted variety of 3 Series flavours was hampering sales potential and you can see a plan coming together.

The result was the E30 3 Series Touring of the late eighties, which was successful and paved the way for a similar 5 Series version. Perhaps the odd thing was that BMW didn't have a 5 Series Touring in mind when it launched the new 5 in 1988. The 3 Series Touring was getting up and at them, but the idea of cooking up a 5 Series Touring was still some time off. Maybe it took all those mid-size wagon sales by BMW's Stuttgart rival to convince it to have a go.

Before getting down to the details, let's clear up one thing about the 5 Series Touring, just in case you have had little chance to

The E34 Touring was proof that niche markets can exist within niche markets! (Courtesy Daniel Srebro)

encounter one. They are not the last word in load lugging. Purge from your mind visions of faux wood panelled seventies Ford Country Squires with weak-kneed 351 cube V8s, think slightly more along the lines of David Brown's sixties DB5 shooting brake and you'll be closer to the mark. BMW's Touring variants have been more about covering the ground stylishly and quickly than having closet space to fit the kitchen sink and everything else you stash in the basement. It's the estate car for the person that never thought they would own an estate car.

The 5 Touring was intended to deliver good looks and good driving. The sloping tailgate and tapered roof section – whilst compromising ability to carry cargo – gave the new estate a profile that let everyone know that this new friend was still part of the 5 Series clan. BMW even almost managed to blend in the traditional C pillar. It was also good to see that it went to the trouble and expense of creating new rear window frames to match the different roof line of the Touring variant. What am I talking about? Just think back to the Volvo 145, Volvo's estate version of the 144 family saloon. Try and remember the rear doors of the estate: the frames were identical to those on the saloon, in spite of the estate's roofline carrying on high and straight. BMW didn't do that!

Looks aren't everything, of course; the Touring talked the talk, but could it walk the walk? BMW's engineers were able to use stiffer suspension settings and the possibility of self-leveling rear

BMW's good looking E34 Touring went on to 1996 MY, including this 518i SE Touring. The E34 Touring was sold alongside the E39 sedan, until the new Touring was ready for 1997. (Courtesy Ray Coldwell)

Shadowing all those Mercedes 4-Matic estates, BMW offered its all-wheel-drive iX system with the E34 Touring. (Courtesy Mark Hoy)

suspension to maintain the handling composure associated with the saloon version. In fact, *Autocar & Motor* felt that the Touring's handling was a notch better than the 5 Series saloon. This was probably because the Touring versions were released later than their saloon cousins. The two to three year lag between the arrival of the saloon and Touring allowed BMW to factor in some extra refinements.

Initially released in late 1991 in 520i and 525i forms, the Touring did incorporate practical elements to accompany its obvious good looks and performance. Borrowing an idea from the past, the new Touring had a split tailgate. For large loads the entire rear door could be lifted up, or if the driver wanted to throw in the odd item at the last moment the rear glass window could be opened separately for quick access. There

was also the optional roof rack system: when combined with the optional roof rail it allowed easy transportation of awkward or bulky items like bicycles and surfboards.

Less practical but quite spectacular was BMW's roof-long, two-piece metal sunroof. The 'double lever sliding roof', to give the device its full title, could manage any combination of tilt, part open or fully open, at the touch of a button. It was like having front and rear sunroofs for the ultimate in night-time star gazing. In spite of the complex-looking roof assembly, the magic roof took up no more headroom than a conventional sunroof. It was the Touring's technical trump card!

BMW TRIES ALL-WHEEL-DRIVE – 525IX

If you don't mind the idea of a BMW estate then what about a

4x4? BMW was, and still is, largely a rear-wheel drive advocate. Once again it couldn't ignore the developments that were taking place around it. Just as Audi, with its svelte Avant, had made the idea of a stylish estate palatable, it had also glamorised the use of four wheel drive in road cars. Subaru had long been a technical pioneer in the application of all wheel drive outside the domain of the Land Rover, but it took Audi to make the four wheel drive appear sexy.

The high profile of the 1980 Audi Quattro and the success of same on the world rally stage generated a level of showroom magnetism that did the VAG group no harm at all. Its effect on sales of BMW and Daimler-Benz was less benign as Audi managed to notch up an increasing number of conquest sales, in Europe and Britain at any rate. It may not be

The E34 Touring kept fast company: note the BMW bike and Porsche 911 in the garage! (Courtesy Ulrich Schade)

All the major tuners got in on the E34 Touring, including Hartge. Birds BMW could supply your all-purpose shooting brake! (Courtesy Hartge)

HARTGE motorsport

FIVE SERIES PROGRAMME

CHANGE YOUR WHEELS FOR A NEW BMW?

Before part-exchanging your BMW, consider the alternative. We can provide *Complete Transformations* for most BMW models since 1978, and also new models via your dealer. Either way, for *Company Car Drivers*, this is the most *Tax Efficient* method of "New Car" acquisition.

You can choose from a set of exclusive *Hartge* wheels, sports suspension, aerodynamic styling systems, sports exhaust, performance transmission and brakes, or a complete *Hartge* engine or cost effective power system. Either separately or as a *Complete Transformation, Hartge* gives you the edge over *"The Ultimate Driving Machine"*. Call us now for your information pack.

Birds *HARTGE*
BMW PERFORMANCE SPECIALISTS
BIRDS (UK) Ltd.
Bridge Works.
Iver Lane.
Uxbridge. Middx UB8 2JF
Tel: (0895) 810850
Fax: (0895) 237171

possible to teach an old dog new tricks, but there was no way BMW or Daimler-Benz was going to sit idly by and watch this trend pass them by. They decided to join in on the 4x4 road car game.

For BMW and the 5 Series this meant the 525iX of autumn 1990, but the story started long before that date. The first seeds were sown as far back as 1981, when work started on creating a 4x4 version of the 3 Series. While Audi had a relatively easy transition to four wheel drive by virtue of starting with a front-wheel drive car, BMW had its work cut out on its route to quattro. It entailed a new front axle, sump, propshaft, rear differential and centre differential. Karlheinz Radermacher, the then boss of R&D, made some correct predictions in those very early days. There would be no differential locks and the power split would be uneven front to rear, with final oversteer retained. However, an auto version never saw the light of day.

The first showroom evidence of BMW's work was the prototype 325i/4, and *CAR* felt that BMW did a better job on the 4x4 front than Audi when the magazine lined up the new three against the market-friendly 90 Quattro. The 325i/4 led to the E34 525iX, but whereas the 3 Series version was a sporty variant, the 4x4 5 Series' targets lay elsewhere. It was simply another version of the mainstream 525i, a car that used four wheel grip to improve handling when the going got slippery. It wasn't about using the extra traction to contain

The E34 Touring's double lever sliding roof – an expensive option on this 525iX Touring. (Courtesy BMW)

A 1995 M5 3.8, with Daytona Violet metallic exterior. The E34 M5 3.8 was the last M5 handbuilt by BMW Motorsport.
(Courtesy Jonathan Baker)

the power of a monster motor. There was the familiar rear biased 37% front and 63% rear power split, further indication that the 5's extra driven wheels were for aiding traction on road instead of mud plugging off road.

Objective measurements gave weight to the conclusion that the 525iX did indeed offer greater control and safety, both in the dry and as conditions became progressively more treacherous. *Performance Car* track tested a 525iX against a regular 525i. The testing, which attempted to isolate the contribution 4x4 made to better car control, showed that the X version could traverse the standardised tests more quickly and easily with its margin of superiority increasing as conditions became more slippery. One could safely extrapolate the result and say that, if more horsepower was on hand, the advantage given by the four wheel drive would have been even more perceptible.

However, it seems that only Audi could make a commercial

success of using four wheel drive as an image enhancer. The all wheel drive 3 and 5 Series didn't set the sales charts alight. They cost quite a bit more than their two wheel drive counterparts and, in the end, not enough buyers felt that the advantages were worth the premium. BMW was not alone in experiencing this sales shortfall as even Daimler-Benz was forced to eventually pull the plug on its 4 matic.

THE ULTIMATE DIESEL MACHINES!

A more successful change in direction for BMW came in the form of diesel. Given that BMW's reputation in recent times was founded on creating feisty sports saloons, it's no surprise that the company was a latecomer in taking the oil burner route. With the 1983 524 td it was a case of better late than never. In the 2.4-litre turbo diesel BMW had a superb diesel motor, the first diesel engine that could deliver anything approaching petrol engine levels of performance and refinement. The trouble was that BMW didn't capitalise on its foray into what was – for it – a brave new world.

Historians could cite the deal that BMW cut with Ford to supply diesel engines for upmarket Lincoln Continentals in the eighties, plus the eventual introduction of the 324d and 524d, but it was all rather too little. It takes quite a lot for a corporate entity to admit to making a wrong turn, but BMW's moved company spokesman, Richard Gaul, to admit it had been a mistake to launch the 324d nearly two years after the 524td. BMW was right to conclude that the ageing 5 Series design needed more of a marketing boost than its E30 little brother, but there was just too much at stake for such a tardy introduction.

As the situation stood, all

The Type D six-speeder in this 1995 M5 3.8 was early to mid 1990s trendy, but also functional fun.
(Courtesy Jonathan Baker)

The ultimate factory roadgoing incarnation of BMW's racing 24-valve Big Six. The S38B38 provided 340 ECE horsepower. (Courtesy Jonathan Baker)

commentators, and BMW itself, were in agreement that the decision to go heavily into catalyst equipped gasoline European variants so early on was a miscalculation. It was essential groundwork for the years ahead but in the short term it meant that BMW missed out on the European eighties diesel boom that Daimler-Benz – with the 2.5 190D – was more than willing to exploit. Fortunately, BMW had the right diesel hardware and, with the E34 5 Series, wasted no time in actually using it. There was a diesel version of the E34, using

the excellent diesel engine from the E28 524td, ready for sale the moment the new 5s were launched in Europe in 1988.

There was room to make a good thing even better, and in 1991 BMW upgraded the M21 turbodiesel by increasing the stroke to gain a mite of displacement and the addition of an intercooler. Yes, that's right, earlier versions didn't have an intercooler! This gave rise to the 115bhp 525td and the more powerful intercooled 143bhp 525tds, two versions that definitely pushed BMW into the

diesel spotlight. Motoring scribes were starting to say that BMW was turning out the finest diesels in the business and that, in the 525tds, the world had perhaps the first diesel that could be called a high-performance car. BMW's diesels were definitely overshadowing offerings from VW/Audi and diesel stalwart Daimler-Benz.

Marketing blunders were also a thing of the past. BMW was putting its new super diesels under the bonnets of E36 3 Series and E38 7 Series cars. Sales opportunities would not be lost this time; it was a case of once bitten, forever shy! Putting aside the obvious benefit of superior fuel efficiency, it seems that the diesel variants lived up to the BMW claim of being ultimate driving machines. *Autocar & Motor* put a 525tds up against the marginally more potent petrol pre-vanos 520i, and pointed out it was the diesel variant that delivered greater driving pleasure.

Regardless of whether it was in gear acceleration, outright performance or general refinement, the diesel car had its nose in front for the whole test. The engine bay was actually encapsulated by a full length floor so that you couldn't see the ground if you peered through the compartment. There was nothing the petrol car could do that the diesel counterpart couldn't. Given the marginal price difference between the two versions, choosing the petrol version over the diesel could almost have been described as foolish! Looking back at the report's picture of the two cars at the petrol bowser, it's hardly difficult to see why turbodiesels have become so popular in Europe and Britain. What could be better than a petrol 5 Series? A diesel 5 Series, of course!

Why stop at using the BMW diesel in BMWs? It wouldn't be long before Range Rovers and Opel Omegas would be motivated by derv-drinking BMW motors. While BMW was watching mainstream market tastes and changing environmental realities, it hadn't forgotten its primary reason for being: the creation of the best sports saloons. Whereas the M535i and M5s of yore usually sauntered in after the world had grown accustomed to the regular 5 Series

Hartge's H5 programme continued with the E34. Like rival Alpina, the H5 could have BMW's full range of gasoline engines. From hotter baby sixes, to the mighty, limo-sourced V12s!! (Courtesy Hartge)

By the 1990s, Dinan was offering turbo kits for M30 E34 535is, and supercharger packages for the E34 540i. Zero to sixty times were in the low fives for both. (Courtesy Dinan)

range, for the E34 the Motorsport tyre torturer would be there at the start of proceedings – well, almost.

HERE COMES THE M5 3.6!

An M5 was in the offing from the start. Not long after the regular versions appeared the 3.6-litre M5 became a permanent 5 Series fixture, both in continental Europe and Britain, although Britain missed out on the M5 Touring. More importantly, the new M5 was a major reworking of the concept of the Motorsport 5 Series and the whole idea of the sports saloon. Other memorable players like the Vauxhall/Lotus Carlton and the Mercedes E500 sat in on a hand or two, but the M5 was a little different again. As technically accomplished as its rivals were, they were still cars which were made sporty by development. BMW took a car that placed sport at the centre and then refined this in a new direction.

The E34 M5 represented BMW balancing model improvement with driver appeal to reach a new level of ability. The 3.6 M5 was going to have a greater performance envelope than previous versions, sell in all the major world markets and stay with manual transmission! Some of the cars the M5 competed against in Europe were virtually unknown in other countries. Buyer tastes and expectations varied tremendously between these markets. Somehow the M5 honed in on the bands of enthusiasts everywhere, whilst complying with national rules. It was alone in its universal appeal.

Apart from the new underlying structure, the M5 had a swag of new goodies. The engine had grown from 3.5 to 3.6 litres by virtue of a 2mm stroke increase. Engine

management was upgraded to Bosch Motronic M1.2 for fuel mix and ignition timing labours. To keep the new motor from being overly frenetic a flap in the intake manifold adjusted intake length, to strike a happy medium between bottom end pulling power and top end thrust. The old TRX rubber and rims were shown the door and room was made for leviathan 17 by 8-inch rims clothed by Michelin MXX2 covers.

The new hoops were definitely worthy of discussion because of their unusual appearance: two-piece items with a five spoke hub and bizzare looking, bolt-on, aluminium, turbine-like covers which, apparently, sent a welcome zephyr of cool air to the brake discs, useful when engaging in heavy battle. More than one person thought they made the new M5 look like it was wearing whitewalls. Given M5s have a street sleeper, low key look, it was possible to mistake the M5 3.6's cooling covers for ordinary plastic wheel trims placed on an ordinary E34. By the mid '80s, the 'M' badge was the most popular accessory sold in West Germany, so auto scepticism was justified.

Returning to the serious stuff the new M5 incorporated BMW's new servotronic power steering and electronic damper control, or EDC. Oddly, the five-speed gearbox turned out to be an overdrive box. While some might have expected a close ratio five-speeder, it should be appreciated that the final drive ratio was an incredibly short 3.91 to one. So things evened out in the end. With a final drive that short, an overdrive box could hardly create unwanted gearing gaps.

It was all quite reminiscent of

the old M1 where BMW combined tall gears with a short final drive to strike just the right balance. Somehow BMW always seems to have the knack of getting the gearing spot on. With the new M5 there was no compromise with in-gear acceleration, and yet the M5 driver could cruise by at 60mph in top with only 2550rpm registering on the rev counter. Road testers, in Europe at any rate, felt the new M5 lacked that magic 'something', although it was difficult to figure out what the shortfall was. Many may have had fond recollections of the older 286bhp E28 M5, perhaps they wished the new car could have retained some of the raw edge of this earlier version. Some may have been making mental comparisons with Italian exotica, and felt the M5 lacked the particular sparkle that these cars possessed.

The trouble with the M5 was that there wasn't anything to directly compare it with. The best contemporary testers could do was locate hotted-up four-doors or dig deeply into their memory recesses to recall the last time they met a Maserati Kyalami. That the M5 3.6 was considered to have missed the target was probably due to the measuring stick testers used, rather than any intrinsic failings the new M5 had. While *CAR*, *Fast Lane* and *Performance Car* planted seeds of doubt in the minds of potential buyers, US testers were rather more enthusiastic about BMW's new super saloon.

Perhaps it does indeed all come down to measuring sticks. If British testers felt the new M5 was a bit flat in comparison to the latest Porsche 911 or Ferrari 328 GTS, then, across the pond, the M5 was treated in a more kindly fashion.

C&D was outspoken – little surprise there – in expressing how positively it felt about the new M5. Back in 1977, it described the then new 630CSi as the most perfect Pontiac Firebird of all time. The magazine may have subconsciously thought that the new M5 was the ultimate reincarnation of the sixties Chevrolet Impala SS! Whatever motivated this thinking there's no doubt that it felt the new M5 was a good thing, not at all lacking in character. John Phillips III laid such notions to rest by mentioning that the M5 idled like a Camaro Z28 with a bracket-racer General Kinetics cam. The instruction that all potential US M5 buyers should take their new jalopy for a spin on the autobahn was the crowning endorsement. *C&D* felt that only then could the true value of the M5 be experienced, otherwise the owner may never know its full potential.

M5 3.8 – BIGGER IS BETTER

If the M5 3.6 was considered to have missed the boat, then all was forgiven with the 1992 M5 3.8. Absolutely no one old enough to remember the 119bhp 1980 255 cubic inch V8 Ford Mustang Cobra could say that BMW's new six-speed 340bhp power team lacked spice! You could marvel at the reduced 0 to 60 time of 5.8 seconds, or the explosive fire power, but wait, there's more. Part of the displacement increase and general rearrangement of affairs was to boost torque and the power spread. 75% of the 3.8's maximum torque of 295 pounds per foot was available at 1800rpm. The extra gear and the extra torque filled any gaps the M5 3.6 may have had in its repertoire.

The bore of the new motor was increased to 94.6mm, and the stroke was kicked out to no less than 90mm, that's over 10mm greater than the bore in the M1's short stroke 3453cc motor. The compression ratio was up half a point to 10.5 to one. Even the trick intake system of the 3.6 edition was reworked. The intake manifold flap that varied intake tract length was always electronically controlled, now it was brought into line with the fuel mix, ignition timing determined by the engine management computer. Everything was channelled to create usable punch.

CAR mentioned, in a 1995 Giant Test with the Jaguar XJR and Audi A8, that there was no single point in the rev range when the BMW 3.8 came on song. Power simply assembled in linear fashion until it became overwhelming, overwhelming the driver's senses, not the M5's chassis or brakes. BMW's electronic damper control was redeveloped into EDC III, and an optional handling pack bearing the moniker Nürburgring was on hand for the discerning few crying out for something a touch sharper. The Nürburgring package involved extra wide 9in diameter rims with wider section rubber, chunkier sway bars, a retuned servotronic helm and a switchable version of EDC that allowed the driver to stick in the super firm setting.

By now the alloys were a more conventional five-spoke pattern and, from 1995 the M5, and other E34s, received the wider winged kidney grille first seen on the V8 E34 variants. The M5's suspension is worthy of special mention. In the past more aggressive suspension packages were accompanied by

a considerable loss of comfort. However, in recent times more and more performance cars are able to use wide section, lower profile rubber and stiffer suspenders whilst maintaining a tolerable ride. The M5 3.8 was just such a car and *Performance Car* remarked that, even on Britain's bumpy bitumen, the firmer Nürburgring setup was still quite accommodating. The same could not be said about the US 528i fettled by Hardy & Beck (H&B), which collected a much harsher ride along with its new-found composure.

The gearchange was also more user-friendly. In spite of having a relatively large, naturally aspirated motor with over 300bhp and considerable torque, shifting remained light. Not the lightness one might associate with a supermini, but certainly not the strain LJK Setright encountered with a manual Ferrari 400i between Teddington and Petworth in 1984. Unfortunately, the M5's servotronic steering shared the gearchange's light character. Even in Nürburgring adjusted form it was too light. If the steering was too carefree then the accelerator pedal action was too uptight. The latter item was definitely on the stiff side. On the whole, the M5 3.8 was easy to use for one so fleet of foot and heavy in substance.

The absence of traction control was not noticeable. The M5 chassis had tremendous grip and the driver was never left in the dark about what this electrifying four-door was up to. The M5 didn't need traction control, and perhaps the world didn't need tuners! In the past the tuners took standard cars to a level that the manufacturer felt was uneconomic, given the

Motorsport division was initially created to oversee BMW's business on the track, but it has grown to be so much more. The importance of having 'halo effect' adjuncts has become so great that Stuttgart rival Daimler-Benz has absorbed AMG to grab some high-performance limelight. (Courtesy Mel Abrahams)

small pool of potential buyers. The M5 3.8 matched or exceeded anything created involving an E34 5 Series, and it carried the bonus of a warranty from BMW! Previous creations like the Alpina B7/B7S offered a level of performance not available from a 5 Series created by BMW.

Now buyers would have to consider even more carefully whether it was worth paying the same or more for an Alpina B10 BI-Turbo or Dinan 535i turbo when BMW's excellent E34 M5 was already available. Modifying any car is a difficult business as everything has to be kept in balance. More horsepower is only useful if it's easily accessible and the engine can maintain high

states of tune for sustained use. Are the brakes and suspension up to the increased power? How does the new package cope with varying road surfaces, traffic conditions and climates? What shape will the modified car be in after five years, or ten years?

The thorny subject of emission control hasn't even been broached, but enough has been said to show what obstacles exist to improving an already able car. Objectively, it could be said that while tuner specials may not offer more performance than the M5, they are even more exclusive in terms of numbers, and some companies allow owners to improve cars they already own. Even so, the fact that BMW is so adept at improving its

own cars makes the life of tuners that much more difficult. When BMW introduced the turbocharged 745i in 1980, many tuners, like Hartge, said that they would leave to BMW the complex task of creating reliable turbo systems.

Considering everything that BMW does and can do, perhaps there's also value in what it chooses not to do. Alpina came up with the Alpina B12 package for the E34 utilising BMW's V12 motor. Karl-Heinz Kalbfell, as chief of BMW Motorsport, commented that while Motorsport could do anything it would not do everything. It was specifically mentioned that the factory V12 would never be matched with the E34 M5. Given that the E34 was the first 5 Series

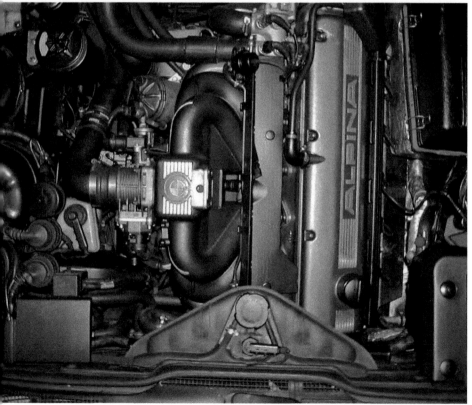

There was an underbonnet switch that allowed the M30 3430cc six to detune itself for regular unleaded. At full tilt it made 384lb/ft at 4000rpm. (Courtesy Alex Wildemann)

to offer 50/50 weight distribution, BMW's restraint becomes partially understandable.

There's also the fact that high speed travel in Europe is becoming increasingly difficult. *60 Minutes* said back in 1994 that its road test trip into the Voges Mountains was hampered by traffic congestion. It was noted that while such an occurrence was unknown when the tests were conducted in the sixties and seventies, it now took almost an hour to cover 20km on the highway. The congestion on the A8 between Stuttgart and Karlsruhe had to be overcome before any spirited mountain road driving.

In October 1987, *What Car?* suggested that the top speed of the new 750iL it was testing had been limited because the tyre manufacturer wouldn't give the green light for sustained speeds above 160mph. There was also a more obvious reason why BMW programmed the ECU to interrupt fuel supply at 156mph. Traffic density, even on unrestricted sections of the autobahn near Hamburg, made reaching even the limited top speed impractical.

From this time on, German car makers reached an agreement to limit the top speeds of their cars in the interests of road safety. The E34 M5 3.6 and 3.8 were both speed limited. Even though magazines stated that their true top speeds wouldn't have been appreciably higher, the self-imposed restraint has symbolic social value in times of environmental and traffic concerns.

Alpina E34 5 Series B10 – an iron
fist in a hand stitched leather glove!
(Courtesy Alex Wildemann)

In a world of compromise BMW seems quite adept at creating possibly the finest four-door sports saloon.

Whilst on the subject of social concerns, the 316g compact and 518g Touring cannot be forgotten. These BMWs marked the development of special Liquified Petroleum Gas – or LPG – M40 engined versions of the E36 3 Series and E34 5 Series. In spite of their relatively restrained performance both models were production cars that investigated the possibility of alternative fuels. Such vehicles are more suitable for countries that have readily accessible reserves of natural gas, such as Australia. There is also the problem of getting the gas to work with a conventional fuel-injection system, and the performance losses noticeable on small displacement engines.

BACK TO V8 POWER

The third generation 5 Series also heralded BMW's return to using V8 petrol engines. In the fifties BMW took the gamble of offering Germany's only, and the world's first, volume produced aluminium V8. It was designed by Alfred Boning and, apart from being made of the light alloy, also featured an in-block oil cooler, but there were a few problems. The motor was quite heavy for the power it produced and the built-in oil cooler wasn't very effective. The hemispherical layout incorporated by Fritz Fiedler on the prewar, 1971cc, ohv straight six wasn't utilised on this new V8 which, apart from its aluminium construction, was quite conventional by postwar, short stroke, ohv, US V8 standards.

While the Boning V8 didn't have the performance measure of the Daimler Benz direct injection, 3-litre, straight six, its real problem was marketing. There was simply too small a market in early postwar Germany for expensive V8-powered BMWs. Even the export markets couldn't help these high class cars pay off. Fortunately, BMW looked to more modest market areas, and came up with the M10 four-cylinder and M30 six-cylinder in the sixties. Both closely related motors were quite excellent and allowed BMW to successfully reach a wide market. Indeed, the M10 was such a cornerstone in BMW's recovery that it was the inspiration behind the company's four-cylinder headquarters in Munich.

One of these two engines found its way into every BMW model released between 1962 and 1988, including the 1972 BMW Turbo show car and the 1978 mid engined M1. Indeed, the M30 was used in cars it wasn't even originally intended for. It was initially designed to power BMW's big saloons and coupés of the late sixties. BMW had planned that the first 7 Series would use the prototype twelve-cylinder

TIGER WITHOUT

A dramatic headline, admittedly.
But then the 3.5 litre Alpina B10 comes from an even more dramatic bloodline.

It is descended from the car you see sitting menacingly in the background: the notorious 'Batmobile.'

A three-times European Touring Car Champion and first embodiment of Alpina's stated aim: to take cars of the highest quality onto an even higher plane.

Based on the already successful BMW 3.0 CSL of the early seventies, the car was nevertheless totally re-built.

Engine, gearbox, suspension, brakes and wheels were re-designed to Alpina's racing specification.

And in the successive hands of Niki Lauda and Dieter Quester, the tiger then set about earning its stripes in no uncertain manner.

Alpina then turned to the urban jungle.

They continued the line in a range of road cars which

engine it was working on in the mid seventies. However, given the sharp rise in fuel prices, this plan was put on hold for quite a few years. In the end, the E23 7 Series finished its days powered exclusively by the M30.

The M30 even gave good service

Two M30 powered bimmers. The younger car, on the left, is an E34 5 Series that has become the recipient of Alpina's 260bhp B10 package. (Courtesy Alpina GB)

in the third generation 5 Series, in spite of the fact that it was already 20 years old by the time the first E34 535is were released. Even so, it remained the only engine used by BMW for the Motorsport editions of the E34 5 Series, and nothing has been heard then or since to suggest it was in any way a mistake.

A big contributing factor to BMW, and others, changing existing engine policy was the introduction of the Lexus LS400 and Nissan Infiniti Q45. These sharp, competitively priced V8-powered luxury cars achieved no less than 181,129 sales up to May 1993 in the US alone.

This development made rivals

sit up and take notice. As Toyota and Nissan were newcomers to this market, it can be safely said that the two Japanese car makers' achievements largely amounted to conquest sales gained from established marques. In any case, it prompted several parties to go away and come up with 3.5- to 4.5-litre, four-camshaft, four-valve, aluminium V8 equivalents. General Motors came out with the Northstar edition, Ford introduced a modular V8, Daimler-Benz made room in its range for a 400E, and BMW was set to respond, too.

It was ironic that BMW, master of niche marketing and well known for having several variants separated by small differences in their engine displacement, had nothing on its shelves to cope with the changing market. As things stood there was nothing between the 3.4-litre M30 six-cylinder and the recently added 5-litre V12 for non-Motorsport bimmers. In the seventies, BMW had worked on prototype V8s and V12s by doubling up on the existing fours and small sixes, but escalating fuel prices meant that BMW actually benefited from sticking to the M30.

After watching rivals suffer in the US as they tried to cope with stricter gas guzzler limits, BMW felt justified in not moving to larger motors with more cylinders. However, since 1986 the world fuel price had started on a downward trend and, as the *Daily Express*' David Benson wrote in that publication's 1987 guide to world cars: "Big Is Beautiful – again." Buyers all over the world, not just North America, wanted larger displacement, naturally aspirated engines.

Jaguar chairman, Sir John

The 286bhp 540i was a luxury sports powerhouse compared to the sports luxury E34 M5. Similar but different, and both sportier than Mercedes and Jaguars. (Courtesy Lee Ridgway)

The new Nikasil 3- and 4-litre BMW V8s had some reliability problems. The coated bores didn't much care for US high sulphur gasoline. (Courtesy Lee Ridgway)

Instead of the M5 3.8, North America utilised the 4-litre V8. Including this Motorsport made Canadian M540i. It combined the 4-litre V8 / six-speed power team, with the 1995 M5 3.8's chassis. (Courtesy Rich Wedenig)

Egan, mentioned that Jaguar was surprised by how bullish demand was for the series three XJ-12. He also added that Jaguar had designed the new XJ40 to utilise only the AJ6 motor, since it was felt that demand for the 5.3-litre V12 would diminish.

It didn't take long for BMW to enter the fray with two new V8s created by joining two of the company's M40 four-cylinder motors at the crankshaft. The new, all-aluminium units arrived in 3 and 4-litre displacements, producing 218bhp and 286bhp respectively. The V8's block weighed just 25 kilos, featured sintered conrods, galvanised bores coated with a nickel deposit, four chain-driven camshafts, four valves per cylinder, and a serpentine belt and pulley system for engine auxilliaries. The plastic intake manifold and motor shrouding, seen on the M50 baby six, was used once again on the

The torque of the all-alloy, 4-litre V8 comes in handy on trackdays! The 4-litre in the E34 540i, and subsequent 4.4-litre version in the E39, have made many friends since the V8's early '90s release. They have worked better with an auto than most previous powerplants fitted to a 5 Series. (Courtesy Dave Brennan and Jack Puryear)

They have convenience equipment similar to rival models from Lexus and Infiniti, but the true mettle of a BMW is revealed out on the open road. (Courtesy Mike Teets)

new V8s to reduce weight, cut noise and mask engine bay clutter.

Introduced as part of the revised 7 Series and 5 Series ranges, in 1992 and 1993 respectively, the new engines put BMW back into the thick of the action. Many motoring publications stated that they gave the E32 7 Series a new lease of life. In 4-litre form, BMW's V8 gave a particularly stirring performance. *Autocar* & *Motor's* twin test of the 4-litre 7 Series and the Lexus LS400 gave results that were not totally unexpected. The BMW V8, whilst the same size and similar in specification, was very different in nature. Compared to the V8s from Lexus, Daimler-Benz, Lincoln and others, the BMW engine still delivered its strongest punch in the higher rev ranges.

It was no surprise that the Lexus LS400 trailed the BMW V8 in acceleration up to 100mph, but from this point the higher drag factor of the older E32 allowed the Lexus to catch up. If the BMW lived up to form by making more horses per-litre, it was also true to form in not being the quietest newcomer to the V8 ranks. Testers and buyers marvel at the silence of the Lexus, but BMW didn't see a need to muffle its new motor completely: yes, it was restrained, but didn't have the stony silence of its competitors. The chance to hear the sporty roar of the new V8 under hard acceleration was a pleasant change after the tomb-like quiet of the Lexus.

BMW's decision to stay true to its traditional character made sense. The Japanese rivals had a level of refinement that pleased the US market, and the potential profit from that part of the globe could hardly be ignored. However, it should be noted that the Japanese cars made a smaller impression, sales-wise, in continental Europe, and Germany in particular. Cars like the Lexus LS400 and Caddy SeVille were available but their characters didn't suit the tastes of German buyers. The attractions of hush and gadgetry didn't excite a country where excellence in chassis, brakes and top end power delivery are of greater worth than the ease with which the standard cruise control can be operated.

So BMW entered the V8 luxury sector, but BMW's take on the concept was noticeably different to that of its competitors. The decision to create a car adaptable to all world markets had merit. In 1994, sales of the Nissan Infiniti were noticeably damaged by US buyers not warming to controversial restyling. It was all reminiscent of what Hermann Winkler, head of BMW exports, had said about the US market back in 1971. He stated that the US was an unstable market and that, at the time, unlike other car makers, BMW's game plan was to tread carefully rather than go for quick expansion in that part of the world.

After the acid test of having the V8s in the 7 Series in 1992, it

If you couldn't afford a 530i/540i V8, go for the look! Thanks to the 5 Series' shared winged kidney, a 520iSE is hard to visually differentiate. (Courtesy Martin)

In SE spec with leather and walnut, this 520i shared the 540i's ambiance. Just exercise that badge delete option!
(Courtesy Martin)

was the 5 Series' turn for 1993. Initially, there were the 530i saloon and Touring, both available with manual or automatic, whilst the 540i was available in auto form only. BMW's official line was that the M5's cog swapper couldn't handle the torque of the 4-litre V8, and it would be uneconomic to have a stand alone manual box for an executive variant that would be ordered almost exclusively as an automatic. The BMW 5 Series was getting bigger and heavier, and

buyers wanted the combination of a large, naturally aspirated engine with the ease of an auto. Even in manual popular Britain, only 25 self-shift E32 735iLs were imported between 1988 and the model's demise in 1992.

All was not lost, however, as the 3-litre V8 editions were available for immediate purchase with manual gearboxes. In a move reminiscent of the 1975 US 530i, BMW decided to buck the trend and go manual again in the States. The 1994 530i

V8 could be ordered in the US with the stick shift. Needless to say, its rivals, as was the case two decades before, were exclusively automatic. There is evidence that more than a few cars were purchased in this form. Only BMW could have gotten away with this trick! Any other manual luxury saloon in the States would have definitely gathered showroom dust.

C&D's Frank Markus suggested that telling the truth about the new 530i V8 could even raise

The 2-litre Single Vanos six achieved 150 silky horsepower. It also fitted in Italy's fiscal 2-litre motoring ceiling. (Courtesy Martin)

public image. Simply state that, in the US 530i V8, you had the most expensive luxury V8 manual saloon in the country. Friends would be in awe, although, of course, you would have omitted the fact that the 530i V8 was also the only luxury V8 saloon in the country! Even more joy was in store because BMW soon introduced a six-speed manual gearbox for use with the 540i. There was a move at BMW to redeploy the 8 series in a more cost-effective sporty light,

and where there was a manual 840i there could also now exist a manual 540i. So, BMW hadn't completely copied the Daimler-Benz preference for auto only in its expensive models.

However, not everything was perfect with the new V8 5 Series as the 530i V8 was a little short on torque. Although BMW's adverts claimed it had more horsepower and better economy than the old 3.4-litre six, it didn't take long to discover that a manual 530i

required more vigorous stirring than the older 535i to keep things on the boil. However, there was no doubt that the new 530i V8 had appreciably more squirt than the, by now defunct, 188bhp E34 530i six-cylinder.

The 4-litre version received no complaints regarding performance. With engines as technically efficient as these, an extra litre of displacement literally works wonders. It implied a reduction in the 0 to 60 sprint of approximately

177

Even on closer inspection, it's hard to distinguish the 520iSE from its upmarket brethren. (Courtesy Martin)

1.75 seconds better than the 3-litre edition. In spite of the sub seven second sprint *R&T* recorded with the US 540i, Andrew Bornhop mentioned that the new V8 lacked the torque-ripe feel of a traditional ohv US V8. Whilst this was partly true, BMW's new V8 – and those offered by rivals – were a different kettle of fish: relatively small in size but technically advanced, with a linear punch of thrust and a level of refinement at high rpm that the older cast iron ohv units could never match.

If the V8's initial response was a mite on the meek side, the driver had only to extend the engine further to get the power that was present. Unfortunately, early V8s inherited the M40's penchant for front crankshaft oil leaks and prematurely worn valve gear. Perhaps some old ghosts from BMW's fifties' V8 had returned to haunt Munchen's latest V8! It was an unfortunate development after the tough M10 and M30.

Whilst on the subject of design, there were a few developments in this period worthy of note. Lexus engineers had discovered that, by carefully selecting the thickness of rubber seals around door frames, they could create a sound when the door was closed that pleased buyers, giving the impression of a solid panel and sturdy latch mechanism. In 1994 BMW's Dr Gerhard Thoma, when commenting on the excellent sound that the 7 Series door made

when closing, noted that, in today's industrial world, sound was less and less a product of chance.

In developing the new V8, BMW engineers discovered that prototype motors emitted an unpleasant sound at between 2500 and 3000rpm. A non-cylindrical camshaft was the answer and the unwanted vibration was gone. While manipulating acoustics helps product planners target a particular group, for example sports variants should have a more vocal exhaust, one must continue to consider the substance rather than the form. Durable mechanicals and quality construction helped BMW quickly achieve international stardom. This largely unseen mechanical bedrock should not be forgotten.

11

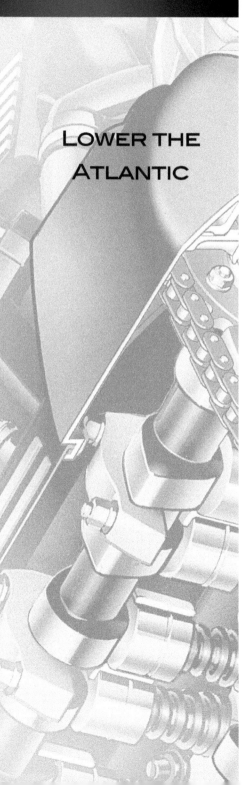

LOWER THE ATLANTIC

"The United States are and will remain BMW's most important market outside Germany." This is a quote from BMW's Dr Robert Buchelhofer, a board member and the then head of Sales and Marketing. For the first time in the Bavarian car maker's history, a new model, the 1992 3 Series coupé, had made its international debut in the United States. In August 1994, Les Bidrawn tested the revised 740i in Munich and noted that BMW repeatedly made it known that it was attentive to the needs and driving style of US customers. It was certainly an about-face compared with Hermann Winkler's view of the US market in 1971.

In economically depressed 1974, BMW achieved a sales record in the US of 15,000 units. By 1989 the sales target for the US was no less than 85,000 units! There was a foot operated parking brake for automatic E38 7 Series cars; who could forget the new, $600 million US dollar manufacturing plant located in the US? Concrete evidence of

A 1989 US 535i sporting 17-inch Borbet rims, Eibach pro kit springs and Bilstein dampers. This was the first year that the E34 5 Series was available in North America. (Courtesy Barry Kaplan)

A 525i auto complete with 'Power Cat,' the mascot of Kansas State University's football team. In motoring, as in sport, the opposition never stands still and BMW has made revisions to the volume-selling small six-powered 5 Series to keep it ahead of the game. (Courtesy Dick Schneiders)

BMW's ever-increasing interest in this large market. Older BMW aficionados find it hard to believe that today in South Carolina there are US assembled BMWs rolling off a production line.

With this background in place we can move onto what the third generation 5 Series was up to in the US. From 1988 onwards, the 5 Series sold in America was converging with the version available in Europe.

The world price of crude oil was on a downward trend, and US government and industry seemed of one mind regarding slackening CAFE programme restrictions for passenger vehicles. Fuel efficiency was less important and stricter EEC guidelines concerning emissions implied that economy and emissions matters were converging in every respect.

The standard E34 impact bumpers were already capable of meeting a 5mph bumper basher test. The 5 Series available in the States was much the same animal as the one on sale in Europe. Indeed, *R&T*'s Ted West noted in 1988 that the new 535i available in Munich was almost identical to the one on sale in Minneapolis. The new US range kicked off with the 525i and the 535i. The 528e had been discarded due to the easing pressure on fuel prices. The 524td was also culled as America

In January 1994, *C&D*'s Frank Markus said the 530i V8 was the best V8 stickshift luxosedan ... and the only one! (Courtesy Robert Kane)

With a 1994 base price of $42,890, the manual was pretty expensive. No one ever said being an enthusiast was easy. (Courtesy Robert Kane)

The E34 M5 3.6 made a 1990 debut at $58,450. Heated front seats cost an extra 250 bucks. Well, at least the radio was standard! (Courtesy Dean Novak)

had gone off diesels by now. Even major diesel market advocate Daimler-Benz was trying to work out how to get its largest, thirstiest petrol motors into US models to satisfy changing times and tastes.

In spite of power ratings for the US 525i, 535i and M5 of 189, 208 and 310bhp respectively, the North American line-up had the same power as Euro editions. Europe's respective ratings of 192, 211 and 315bhp were due to the DIN rating system, whereas America used SAE net figures. They were the same unleaded, cat-friendly motors. More importantly, the new US E34 M5 3.6 didn't suffer from the M88-to-S38 power gulf that its E28 predecessor endured. That is, 286bhp DIN versus 256bhp SAE net.

These were halcyon days for the 5 in the US. With the E34, BMW had a larger, more refined model better suited to US conditions without consciously pandering to US market tastes.

It was quite a relief to US BMW fans. Since the late '60s, national restrictions had prevented them receiving the full strength version of BMW's sporting flavour. The

The M5's reputation increasingly preceded it, and still with no direct Stateside rival ... A four-door Corvette? A 911 for the family, perhaps? (Courtesy Dean Novak)

absence of compromise proved a welcome change. I can cheerfully relay that *C&D* results showed that the new M5 stomped on the 300ZX Turbo, Mercedes 500 SL and contemporary ohv Vettes. Plus, the Infiniti Q45 was shown a clean pair of heels when it came to sprinting to 60 and running through the quarter mile.

With expanding performance came greater choice. In the seventies there was a single US 5 Series, in the eighties there were usually two. Now the range expanded to include a line-up more representative of the European range. There was the 525i, the 530i, touring versions, and the 540i. The 4x4 version of the 525i was never available and the 530i touring was available in automatic only. As usual, US 5 Series versions were well equipped with twin airbags, leather seating, polished walnut, and electric telescopic adjustable steering column on the 540i. However, the lack of climate control air con on the 530i was slightly amiss. With a $42,890 sticker price, it was a surprise to see slider controls and rotary dials present with the 530i's standard HVAC system.

Wherever the market, the M5 3.6's S38B36 motor spelt 310 SAE net horses at 6900rpm, and 265lb/ft at 4750rpm.
(Courtesy Mel Abrahams)

BMW LOCKS HORNS WITH LEXUS

When tested against the E320 wagon and Volvo 850 Sportwagon Turbo, the 530i touring came off third best in the sprinting department. However, *Motor Trend* noted that what the small V8 lacked in scat was more than compensated for by its fine manners. Spare a thought for the old M30 six-pot; 1994 was the first year in 25 years that BMW's big six was absent from the US market. *C&D* nicknamed the M30 'panzer powerplant.' I urge enthusiasts to seek out *Consumer Union*'s 1990

test featuring the BMW 535i, Lexus LS400, Infiniti Q45 and the Lincoln Continental.

The test symbolised the past, present and future of the US luxury car scene. It looked like a walkover for the ultra modern Japanese saloons featuring quad cam, four-valve, all alloy V8s of 4 and 4.5 litres. How could BMW's six-cylinder from the sixties, in two valve single cam form, contending with current US emissions laws and low octane unleaded, possibly keep up with this technical new wave? Actually, it did rather well. The 7.9-second nought to sixty sprint was on a par

with the Lexus, and not far behind the 7.1-second time recorded by the larger displacement Infiniti.

Consumer Union noted that the BMW 3.4-litre six didn't idle as smoothly as the Japanese duo, but didn't embarrass itself either when it came to sheer go. While BMW never let its guard down when it came to spirited mechanicals, not everything was remaining constant. Up until the late '80s BMWs of all kinds had an unusually high stick shift order rate in the US market. Even some of the US 733is laid on for the motoring press at Laguna Seca in 1978 had a four-speed

In 1992, Motorsport boss Karl-Heinz Kalbfell said "We can do anything, but we won't do everything." He said no to an E34 M5 V12! (Courtesy Dean Novak)

floor shifter. As we moved into the '90s a change was in the air. In 1989 *Motor Trend*'s Bob Nagy mentioned that the transmission choice was expected to run 80% auto for the 5's third visit to the US.

The BMW official who spoke to Les Bidrawn was correct, too; there would be no V8 manual 7 Series reaching US shores. However, let's not forget that the 530i could be had with a manual, and ditto for

the 540i as of 1995. We should also be grateful that BMW North America poured cold water on Munich's original plan to offer the 3.6-litre M5 with a zombie shift! No need to reason out why, just be

BMW Motorsport wanted to offer an automatic version of the E34 M5 3.6. Thankfully, BMW North America said no. The E34 M5's sporty reputation remained unsullied. (Courtesy Dean Novak)

happy it didn't try! BMW's choice for US versions was less restricted than ever. With a subdued CAFE and a fuller product line that encompassed an expanded sales base of fuel-conscious 3 Series, the product mix could be adjusted at will.

Both the M5 and the manual 540i incurred the gas guzzler tax, but these were different times and the sum total still placed BMW on the fairway rather than in the bunker. In fact, even though the manual 540i was hit with a $1300 surcharge and

E34 M5 was the first M5 to feature Extended Leather – a concept first seen on the US spec E24 L6 and E23 L7, plus South African 745i. That is, putting leather wherever one can think of! (Courtesy Dean Novak)

was more expensive than the 540i auto, BMW still undercut the Lexus LS400 and Infiniti Q45 on base sticker price.

C&D discovered that the manual shift 540i cut over a second off the sprint to sixty compared with the auto. At 5.7 seconds the BMW was only 0.3 seconds behind the Pontiac Firebird Trans Am SD-455 that C&D tested at Orange County International Raceway in 1973.

It should be remembered that the Trans Am was not air conditioned and couldn't transport four people at 140mph-plus in the comfort and refinement possessed by the BMW. It should also be noted that the BMW achieved all of the above whilst meeting the ever-tightening emission laws of the mid nineties.

If there was one area that could have stood improvement it was the 5 Series' V8 suspension settings. Britain's *CAR* noted that what amounted to an M-Technic package for a 525i didn't do justice to the 540i's power pack, and that it limited the V8's performance envelope. Once again, though, if the present dish lacked salt BMW had a back-up recipe that satisfied the more discerning palate.

THE 540I SPORT REPLACES US M5 3.6

The US never got the 3.8-litre M5, so to balance the scales of justice BMW North America received the 540i Sport. It was an amalgam of the torquey, 4-litre, V8 with the suspension, front rotors and rim combo from the M5. It took advantage of the fact that the 282bhp, 4-litre and six-speed manual package was already EPA emissions certified, and combined this with more accomplished hardware. The standard 540i already came with special front spoiler ducts to channel cool air to the front brakes, but this 540i offered so much more. It was symbolic of a new era for BMW, where Motorsport associated variants would no longer be solely built in Germany. Unfortunately, it has also sparked heated debate amongst bimmer fans of what constitutes a real M car.

Whereas the standard US 540i had a top speed limited to 129mph, the sport version was left to its own devices up to the customary European limit of 155mph. Long gone was the memory of the 85mph speedo, or the bumper bars that some found ungainly. It took the best part of 25 years, but after all this time there finally was convergence.

By the end of 2016 model year, 7.6 million 5 Series had been built. One million of those had been sold in North America, and around only 50,000 of those were E12s. It shows how that continent has become a bigger part of the 5 Series, and BMW business in general, over the years.

A 1993 model year E34 M5 3.8 5 speed. (Courtesy BMW)

12

FORGING AHEAD – BMW UNLEASHES THE NEW E39 5 SERIES

Back in 1974, when *Which?* met the 5 Series for the first time, it had trouble categorising it. The 2-litre engine size and four to five seater saloon body seemed to put it in the Rover 2000, Triumph 2000 class. However, the BMW 520 had a hefty 3500 pounds sterling price tag, just a shade under what a Jag XJ6 cost! The answer was that the new 5 was both cars: a middle order prestige car like the Rover and Triumph, but with even wider technical possibilities and international marketing potential. Potential that was indeed realised in the years to come. BMW had built a better mouse trap!

This rental 520d had 136bhp and 206lb/ft. Diesel variants were on the rise in 1990s Europe, based on great economy and perceived 'green' credentials.
(Courtesy Ulrich Thieme)

BMW solved that sticky bore coating problem, by going from M60 3-litre and 4-litre Nikasil V8s, to the E39's M62 3.5-litre and 4.4-litre Alusil V8 family. (Courtesy Jim Levandoski)

International tastes are one thing, but if something doesn't work it quickly gets discarded. Ronald Barker, writing for *CAR* in 1984, mentioned that it wasn't possible to sit in a summer Tokyo traffic jam with the air-conditioning running in earlier Jaguars without boiling the engine coolant. He added: "So much for all the tales manufacturers tell us journalists about all the R and D in native laboratories and the marathon testing of prototypes in every extreme of climate ..." BMW, and its German rivals, were closer to the truth when it came to R&D fact and fantasy.

Cars like the 5 Series would achieved limited success if the engineers overlooked the detail, an important part of allowing versions, like the E39, to mean more things to a greater number of people. First driven by the world's motoring press in late 1995, the E39 was the fourth generation in the 5 Series line. Its new appearance perpetuated another recent BMW trait: the ability to look more cutting-edge than its rivals. Indeed, it seems the only time a BMW shape becomes dated is when the new version wafts along.

Gone was the E34's shoulder-padded, power dressing image. In its place was a more organic, integrated and rounded creation. The E34 5 Series was often mistaken for the E32 7 Series. This time around, folks were confusing the new 5 with the smaller E36 3 Series, because of similar tail treatment. *CAR* felt that the A pillar ran uncomfortably into the bonnet's power bulge crease, whilst others considered the E39 a touch on the bland side. However, in universal terms it was generally agreed that the new 5 very much looked the part of conservative, yet aggressive and modern, executive express.

This 1997 528i has been modified using Jim Conforti's Shark Injector performance software and H&R springs/Bilstein shocks. It has also been updated with a 2001 model year grille and clear turn signal covers, another popular aftermarket product of recent times. (Courtesy Alex Selamat)

The E39's satellite navigation, based around GPS and CD stored maps, was new to the 5 Series. (Courtesy BMW)

MULTI-LINK & STEPTRONIC

The newbie also brought along some toys. The E39 became the first volume produced saloon to use aluminium suspension: the front/rear subframes, wheel location members; if you were wearing alloys it added up to a 65 kilo weight reduction! Plus, BMW finally ditched the rear semi-trailing arms for a multi-link rear end. BMW's Z arm system was first seen on the Z1, followed by the E36. Now it was the 5's turn for a change.

However, at the front things stayed the same. The space-efficient MacPherson struts were still present. The double pivot lower end once again helped deal with the compromises incurred by MacPherson struts, through improving kingpin axis geometry. Six-cylinder petrol-engined E39s experienced a first for a 5 – rack and pinion steering. Recirculating ball was once the sole choice, but that was now limited to the new V8 petrol and six-pot diesel variants where space constraints permitted nothing else.

By this point in time most of the mechanical and electronic advances that have allowed cars to perform better, and be easier to live with, had already occurred. Thus, it was no surprise that the focus of the E39 was on convenience and driver information facilities, such as the introduction of the multi-function steering wheel first seen on the 1994 E38 7 Series. Having the autosound and cruise buttons on the tiller reduced the clutter of centre consoles swamped by a legion of similar looking buttons.

Then there was the possibility of a dash television monitor which could serve three purposes: watching commercial television; a menu option screen; a map aid tied in with the car's Global Positioning System receiver. Computer CDs would contain the map details of an area and, by following the voice commands conveying direction and distance, you would never get lost again – hopefully! Before getting carried away with technology, let it be known that this gadget listed as a 3950 pound sterling option on a British market 5 Series by March 2001.

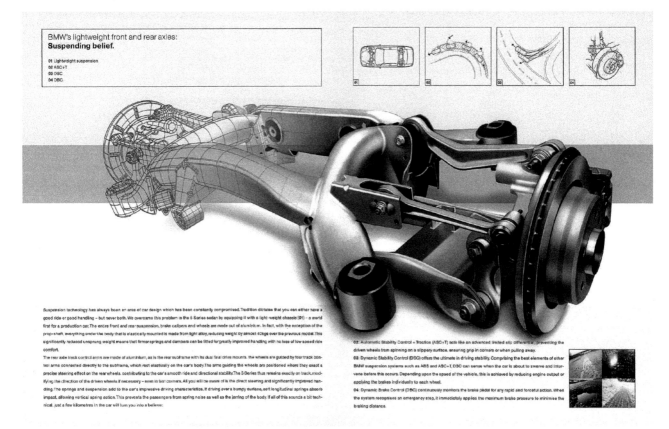

The E39's multi-link rear suspension was a first for the 5. (Courtesy BMW)

Options such as leather-trimmed 'comfort seats' and climate control air-conditioning were available on lower line European E39 models, but were very expensive. (Courtesy Paul Baylis)

BMW returned to conventionally mounted rear safety belts after the reverse setup on the E34 5 Series. (Courtesy Paul Baylis)

That trip computer was back, too, except now there were basic and deluxe versions. Moving down the console, on automatic cars the eyes would alight on the new Steptronic sport shift quadrant. In the mould of Porsche's and Audi's Tiptronic, this gadget added spice to what was a conventional torque converter slushbox. Knock the shifter to a side plane and deft touches forward or back would bring sequential style shifts. The craze for such larks started in 1986 when Jaguar introduced its J-gate on the XJ40.

Steptronic wasn't always an automatic inclusion with the five-speed autobox – it was an option on five-speed auto six-cyl E39s, under the 528i. Indeed, the range still included a starter four-speed auto, which Steptronic wasn't available with, and it was this base autobox that came with US 528is until the close of the 1990s. It gave the US 528i auto a 0-60mph time just north of 8 seconds. For the manual Euro 528i, it was a little south of 7 seconds.

There was a new departure in seating. The E39 gave three possibilities: the standard seat; the more aggressively shaped and bolstered sport seat, and finally the comfort seat. The final of this trio had more of everything, more material, size, padding and price. Such indulgence carried an itemised value of 2195 pounds sterling when the E39 was first launched. For the first time since the E12, the power window controls were back on the door trim panel and the E34's power seat control buttons continued at the base of the front seats.

For HVAC concerns the E39 involves two possibilities. Low

The E39 M5 was the only E39 V8 with Double Vanos. Due to high sales volume, this M5 came off the regular 5 Series production line. (Courtesy Jason Tang)

BMW ALPINA B10 3.3
The entry into ALPINA's 5-series programme

end versions could still sport a triple rotary dial arrangement, which was integrated but lacked full automation and required the operator to push a snowflake button to activate the air con. Or there is the upscale, fully automatic, electronic display setup with two temperature displays for each half of the car. The latter is the one most likely to be found on British market cars and you wouldn't see the former at all on US E39s.

On the detail front the E39 returned to the E28 style, conventional opening bonnet supported by gas struts. The pendulum had swung once again to weight saving. Gone also were the reverse mounted rear seatbelts of the E34 and E36, a small detail but I could sense you wanted to know! The dashboard and instruments stayed true to form: good quality materials and a raised instrument cluster with oversized speedo and tach. The service indicator system and fuel gauge built into the lower half of the tach were still present, even if the intense interest in economy that had led to their development had largely evaporated. They had both become part of BMW's corporate furniture.

The glovebox still featured a rechargeable torch and the boot mounted tool kit wasn't forgotten, even if it was greatly downsized from previous versions. Think of its presence as largely symbolic; people would complain if it wasn't there! After so many years people had expectations of what a 5 Series should encompass. A kidney grille, circular lamps, a firm but comfortable ride and a large number of versions to cater for a variety of tastes. With models ranging from the humble four-cylinder 520d turbodiesel to the mighty 400bhp M5, the E39 didn't disappoint.

of high-temperature-resistant ENGELHARD-coating illustrate this technology

As an entry into ALPINA's 5-series programme the BMW ALPINA B10 3.3 addresses sporty drivers who prefer manual shifting. It is available in manual form only and thus constitutes an interesting counterpart to the B10 V8 whose transmission comes exclusively as a 5-speed automatic with ALPINA SWITCH-TRONIC

The turbine-like revving of the 3.3 litre engine and the complete lack of vibrations in the upper rpm range make comfortable, smooth city cruising in the upper gears just as enjoyable as using the entire bandwidth of speed and power. The BMW ALPINA B10 3.3 accelerates in only 6.3 seconds from 0 to 100 km/h (touring 6.7 seconds), manages one kilometre with dead start in 26.5 seconds

(touring 26.9 seconds) while achieving a top speed of 262 km/h (touring 256 km/h)

In view of this driving performance, consumption of the new six-cylinder appears in a rather favourable light

According to the EC norm, the 3.3 litre saloon only needs 10.2 litres/100 km; the touring,

weighing 100 kg more, merely needs 0.1 litres more. The B10 3.3 thus proves the importance ALPINA places on environmental aspects and sets a prime example for what can be achieved with the most advanced technology. The highly sophisticated twin-scroll exhaust system with stainless-steel elbow joints, heated lambda probes and catalysts whose EMITEC metal substrates dispose

Alpina's custom 3.3-litre version of BMW's double Vanos baby six. (Courtesy Alpina GB)

The E39 came out with the lowest drag factor of any 5 Series to date; some versions went as low as 0.27. The use of all-aluminium suspension was a first for a volume produced saloon. (Courtesy Ed Becker)

EURO E39 VARIANTS

Mainstream tastes are served with six-cylinder petrol models like the 520i, 523i and 528i, although with European petrol prices and the rise and rise of the turbodiesel, this may not be the case forever. Anyway, the six-pot petrol variants putting out 150bhp, 170bhp and 193bhp come closest to satisfying most of the motoring needs of worldwide BMW purchasers. Engine sizes and power levels still reflect European fiscal restrictions that affect the cost of motoring.

All six-cylinder variants feature a development of the M60 baby six which was launched back in 1977. From 1999 MY, M52TU six-cylinder E39s have an all-aluminium motor, twin cams, four valves per cylinder and double Vanos. (The last item involves using variable valve timing for both the intake and exhaust valves, a development on the earlier Vanos setup that looked at the intake side alone.) Please note that BMW has increasingly chosen to diverge from its series, engine

The revamped and enlarged 3-litre in the 530i offers considerably more horsepower than the preceding, fiscally restricted 2.8-litre 528i. (Courtesy Ronald Rogari)

capacity model indentification system. Thus, the 523i and the 540i are actually powered by a 2.5-litre six and 4.4-litre V8 respectively, confusing and illogical but true!

The 520i is really a European based variant. Its reduced displacement makes manual transmission essential for good performance and economy. Such a power team can produce a top speed of over 130mph, 0 to 60 in a shade under ten seconds and a touring range of 450 miles from

In European specification the E39 530i is a genuine 150mph saloon, the perfect choice for safely travelling on continental auto routes at high speeds. In fact, this particular car was purchased using the European delivery programme.
(Courtesy Ronald Rogari)

sale in the US as a 2001 model year variant. In today's motoring scenario, journalists say that the question is no longer whether to buy a 5 Series, but more a case of which one?

The consensus of opinion seems to come down on the side of the six-cylinder manuals. Their optimal weight distribution, rack and pinion steering, easy to shift, light, manual gearboxes make them the nearest thing to automotive utopia. The five-speed autobox BMW uses is excellent in terms of shift quality and driving range options, but doesn't combine as well with the six-cylinder cars as does the stick shift. Within this selected range the final decision of the automotive judges sees the manual 528i, and its successor, the up-engined 530i, as the last contestants standing. Manual six-cylinder E39s use the same five-speed box with a direct one-to-one fifth; from here BMW plays with the final drive to get the balance right.

The range is a tall 2.93 to 1 for the 528i to a short 3.46 to 1 for the 520i. While that may sound like too many revs in top for comfortable cruising, it should be noted that German drivers like having flexible top gear acceleration. It allows the car to stay on cam for a greater speed range and disposes of the need for frequent downshifts for passing or encountering mild inclines. A 5 Series is a German car, and German buyers have always wanted cars that can be driven as fast as the road and conditions permit. This involves cars designed to operate and cope with continued high speed travel. If there seem to be a few more revs than there should be, don't worry, it was designed to work that way!

the 520i's 70-litre tank. With a compression ratio of eleven to one, higher than the 523/528, the E39's 0.27 drag factor and the already mentioned weight saving from the use of aluminium, what the 520i lacks in quantity it makes up for in quality.

Now that the 518i has departed

the 520i makes a competitive entry level European 5 Series model. However, for something of a more international blend, look to the larger motored 523i and 528i. With their appreciated boost in torque these versions are closer to a happy medium. In fact, a revised version of the 523i, the 525i, has gone on

BMW's Double Vanos, with variable valve timing on intake and exhaust sides. It was fitted to all petrol sixes from 1999 MY, as the M52TU. (Courtesy BMW)

While the 5 Series was staying faithful to its national and model character, the engineers were working towards a variation of the same thing. At first glance the 170bhp 523i looked like a comedown from the 192bhp E34 525i. The truth was that the newer E39 had a better spread of useable power, and managed to eke out better in-gear and outright performance, plus better economy. BMW used Double Vanos to make the most of the available displacement, managing to build up 180 pounds per foot of torque at a touch under four grand and max power at a relatively leisurely 5500rpm. The E39 bettered every figure in the book compared to the E34, in spite of the fact that the newcomer was physically larger and had more interior space, most noticeably in the back seat.

Autocar discovered that a manual 528i could combine a 142mph top speed, a 0 to 60 sprint in 6.8 seconds and good fuel economy. The April 1996 test pointed out that rival cars couldn't achieve such a balance, especially when throwing criteria like ride comfort and handling into the equation. In fact, when all the calculations were done, the 528i proved more frugal than it's little brother, the 523i. The shorter final drive ratio had extracted a penalty at the pump. With all this goodness on tap any minor reservations that the 2.8-litre motor lacked the response of the torque-oriented 2.5-litre seemed marginal.

I hear you want more? Well, you've got it! BMW had finally upgraded its standard level of equipment for continental European and British markets. In Britain, where right-hand drive requirements and transportation helped fudge the issue of value for money, there is no doubt that, pound-for-pound, British buyers paid much more for their bimmers. To charge extra for a radio, and a lockable glove box on top of that was really trying it on.

This 2002 530i Sport six-cylinder could do 0-60mph in 6.5 seconds, and reach 150mph. (Courtesy Peter Thorpe)

Car makers often adopt popular aftermarket items for their product lines. The clear turn signal covers and 17-inch alloy rims with staggered rubber came from the factory. There are so many BMW alloy rim designs to choose from today that they have number codes. (Courtesy Paul Baylis)

The 3-litre double Vanos inline six is a versatile motor, used in a number of markets and several BMW models. There are versions of the 3 and 5 Series, plus the X5, which feature this high output petrol unit. (Courtesy Ronald Rogari)

At least with the E39, buyers were getting a decent level of standard equipment. The 1997 520i SE came with climate control air con, alloys and stereo, even if it still looked a bit spartan compared to the gadget-laden Saab 9-5 2.0i SE, which, I might add, undercut the 520i by one thousand pounds sterling!

Standard alloys were an attractive, deep dished style in a 15 by 7-inch rim. Optional, and frequently fitted to the 528i, were more elaborate 16 inchers.

M-Technic sports pack suspension was a worthwhile option which sharpened up the already good E39 suspension without adversely affecting the composed ride. It was money well spent. When judging such an equipped E39 it could be said that, whilst the whole package lacked the directness and steering feel of the older E34, here was a ride/handling/refinement combination on a different level. BMW updated the 5's traction control so that it was now known as ASC. You could still turn it off and

recent years had seen such devices become even less intrusive. There's nothing worse than the big brother feel to ruin a spirited driving experience.

BMW hasn't forsaken handling ability in favour of firepower under the bonnet and pipe smoking by the hearth. Autocar's twin test involving the BMW 520i and Saab 9-5 revealed the true hero on a challenging section of bitumen. For the most part the Saab drew level in achieving good ride comfort, but when the going got

The closest thing to an E39 M5 in the BMW stable: the 2003 US 540i M-Sport. All E39s had exterior styling by Joji Nagashima. (Courtesy Bill Johnson)

Unlike the M5, the 540i M-Sport could have an autobox. However, this particular ride possesses a six-speed stick shift. (Courtesy Bill Johnson)

On the trivia front, the E39 saw the return of a conventionally opening bonnet. BMW's boot mounted tool kit was still present, albeit in downsized form as a token reminder of the past. Thankfully, BMW has resisted giving the E39 a foot operated parking brake. (Courtesy Ed Becker)

tough it was the BMW that got going. The Saab bottomed out on one part of the chosen test course; the 520i was less perturbed. It was all reminiscent of a day in 1978 at Laguna Seca when BMW North America revealed the new US 733i to interested parties. Patrick Bedard of *C&D* sampled one of the 733s on hand and found it more than equal to the task of coping with the infamous Corkscrew.

V8 E39S – 535I & 540I

So, if the six-cylinder E39 is so good, where does that leave the V8 version? Somewhere different, would have to be the answer, not better or worse, just different. BMW's audience is expanding all the time, it has to for BMW to remain economically viable and generate enough cash to reinvest and create good future models. Some markets prefer large engined automatics. More than a few folks chose an auto, but would still have liked some zotts under the hood. For many it would be plain bizarre to find a cylinder count of less than eight in such an exalted price range. Then again, who said you even need a reason to choose an E39 V8? Perhaps you just like the car? If you do, what's the deal?

Models under consideration are the 535i and 540i V8, both of which feature developments of the quad cam, four valves per cylinder, all-aluminium V8 first seen on the E32/E34. The old 3- and 4-litre units were replaced with 3.5 and 4.4-litre updates that focused on even torque delivery, a sore point with smaller versions. The

After years of using the semi trailing arm rear end, the E39 introduced multi-link rear suspension to the 5 Series, plus rack and pinion steering. (Courtesy Ed Becker)

new motors did cure the pokey response, and when teamed with the manual gearbox with direct fifth the 535i was a force to be reckoned with. The only trouble was that, with a small sprinting margin and academic advantage in top speed, the manual 535i didn't offer much over the manual 528i: it was a whole lot of dough for slightly better go.

The foibles didn't stop there, either. The manual five-speed available with the 535i or the six-speed available – even in the US

– for the 540i, lacked the precise shifter feel and light clutch action of the six-cylinder E39s. So that means you should get the autobox, right? Well, yes and no. The five-speed Steptronic box had lots of gears and the V8s had lots of torque, but something was missing. It was that pause between shifts that even the best autos can't overcome, the laboured feel of extra electronic attention expended to select the right cog. It's hard to explain, but the manual sixes are a hard act to follow when it comes to sporty feel.

To overcome this problem it's necessary to head to Alpina and purchase the auto only, yes, you heard right, Alpina B10 4.6 E39. This beasty with a Switchtronic-fettled version of BMW's five-cog Steptronic permits rich buyers to play with the gears using steering wheel mounted buttons. It was what the naked eye couldn't see that made the real difference. Alpina had massaged the engine management software to allow its unique version of BMW's V8 to rev to 7000rpm. It was a key element

BMW's Steptronic facility gives the choice of sequential shifts from a conventional torque converter autobox by knocking the shifter sideways into a special gate. (Courtesy Ronald Rogari)

in virtually eliminating gearchange delay. That's all well and good if you can afford an Alpina, but what about the regular V8?

BMW Car's Charles Armstrong-Wilson, when driving the 520i and 540i back-to-back, echoed the sentiment that the regular V8 had a gearchange delay stick shift lovers would find hard to live with. On the positive side, the Steptronic facility did allow the driver to stay in one gear indefinitely: handy when trying to maintain a particular line whilst charging hard through a corner. However, the sort of driver that performs such manoeuvres would probably be happier with a manual car. As sophisticated as the five-speed autobox BMW uses undoubtedly is, it is still a torque converter automatic. The same style as the majority of the world's autos, the same as that first Dynaflow unit wielded by Buick in the late forties.

The principle has stayed the same; use the action of moving vanes of fluid to transfer energy from the engine, with the bonus of the torque converter's amplification up to a certain roadspeed that eliminates the need for one gear when compared to a manual box. You get the smoothest auto shifts but there are trade-offs regarding efficiency and immediacy. However many electronics you cram into one of these units you can't overcome the laws of physics – it looks like we will be making compromises for some time to come. Beyond the auto's idiosyncrasies there is the recirculating ball steering of the E39 V8.

As with past 5 Series generations the tiller has a slightly dead feel at about the straight ahead area. The

High-Tech and Quality of Life

It has never been our goal to produce a race or rallye car for the road. Instead, we intend to combine ecological aspects, i.e. economical consumption and excellent emission levels, with sheer driving pleasure, thereby augmenting the quality of life with our automobiles

When producing automobiles it is our task to make sure driving is and stays one of the most beautiful and rewarding experiences for many people

In accordance with this philosophy we started thinking years ago about how driving an automatic could become even more dynamic and sensible by the active intervention of the driver, without having to compromise on the comfort and quality features of a modern automatic

The final outcome of these thoughts is ALPINA SWITCH-TRONIC, developed in a joint effort with ZF and BOSCH, representing an electroniccontrol for the ZF automatic gearbox in BMW ALPINA automobiles. The two driving programmes, Automatic and SWITCH-TRONIC, constitute the ideal basis for this driving style in any kind of situation

The automatic-programme offers a perfectly matched programme for relaxed automatic driving, changing gears according to driving style, torque and performance characteristics. Additionally, a more dynamic driving style is possible without having to resort to the use of kickdown

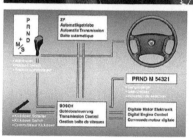

changes gears deliberately in the same way as he would with a manual gear, thus always having an active and own choice of gear

In this way, the advantage of engine braking can be used, it can be downshifted prior to entering a bend, and the gear can be fixed when driving on mountain roads so that unnecessary shifting up and down is avoided. Because a

When selecting the SWITCH-TRONIC-programme, the gear currently in use is fixed. By touching one of the two switch buttons integrated into the reverse side of the steering wheel, the driver can shift up or down using the right and left buttons, respectively

The shift in gear comes immediately and without interruption of traction force. The gear is then held until the driver chooses another gear by switching at the steering wheel - as with the 'Formula 1' semi-automatic gearboxes. Therefore, the driver

gear can be selected immediately regardless of throttle position, the car can be accelerated without delay, important in overtaking manoeuvres where lifting the throttle on approaching the vehicle in front would produce an upshift in an ordinary automatic. Whilst in SWITCH-TRONIC mode, the torque converter lock-up clutch is normally closed, producing the minimum of power loss through the converter

The system's electronic controls also have the following fail-safes to assist the driver:

– upshifts occur automatically at the revolution limit
– manual downshifts are ignored by the system, if this would lead to engine overrevving
– upon slowing to a halt, 2nd gear is automatically selected. A manual downshift to 1st gear is possible, if maximum acceleration from standstill is required
– the kickdown function is maintained and always has

priority to prevent possible wrong-shifting

ALPINA SWITCH-TRONIC thus offers the ultimate solution for driving an automatic in the most efficient, convenient, and responsive way possible. It inevitably adds a wholly new dimension to the conventional driving experience: once you have experienced it, you no longer want to drive without it

Alpina's Switch-tronic software involves upping the engine redline and revised programming to reduce the lag between shifts. The general consensus is that the system works well in eradicating the slightly lethargic feel of the standard automatic. (Courtesy Alpina GB)

real bugaboo is that the unit used in the E39 just plain can't match the precise feel of the rack and pinion system used on the nimbler six-cylinder cars. Of course, in the more luxury focused US such critical thinking has less weight. The 528i, with a sticker price of $38,900, and the $49,900 540i entered North America as 1997 model year cars. In the US that's considered a great deal of bread to spend on a car. The models sported 190bhp and 282bhp (SAE net) versions of the European engines.

In this market bedecked luxo

5s were right on target with local tastes. BMW, as ever, had the knack of making the right compromises. US buyers who used to buy Cadillacs, Lincolns and Imperials often choose German luxury marques today. The same situation exists in the British market where BMW, Daimler-Benz and Audi dominate the prestige saloon segment. This has occurred in spite of buyers turning away from saloons in general, as with the once popular but now defunct European Ford Granada.

2001 saw the E39's first facelift

and the introduction of the 525i and 530i, largely taking over from the 523i and 528i. The 523i and 525i both have 2.5-litre engines, but the 530i has a new 231bhp, 3-litre version of BMW's small six. New Sport variants add spice to the line-up with their firmer suspension and monster rim/tyre combination. Rims that resemble M5 refugees, measure 17 by 8 inches at the front and 17 by 9 inches at the back. The facelift consisted of clear glass headlamps, with an illuminated outer ring once on dipped beam, a bolder kidney grille and revised

A car which combines dynamic performance with stunning looks, the new BMW 5 Series has the very essence of BMW to present you with the new benchmark performance saloon car.

The 523i actually had a 2.5-litre six, not a 2.3-litre unit as the model designation suggests. Britain's Princess Diana became the first UK E39 5 Series owner, with an order placed for a 1996 528i. (Courtesy BMW)

BMW ALPINA B10 V8
Reconcilliation of running smoothness and power

Throughout ALPINA's 30-year history its cars have been known for their exceptional performance. That much is taken for granted. But over this period BMW ALPINAs have evolved, taking advantage of, and improving upon, the technology of the time. And not just in the pursuit of more power. Improving performance is only one part of ALPINA's philosophy. The company is constantly developing and honing its cars. The ALPINA customer is an enthusiast who appreciates high technology and seeks great driving pleasure from his car, yet prefers a car more refined and more practical than today's sports cars. A BMW ALPINA is high performance in a most subtle guise

The B10 V8 is one example in a long line of BMW ALPINAs produced using the company's philosophy and attention to detail. It builds upon the outstanding qualities of the BMW 5-series in a way that only a specialist car maker like ALPINA can

At the heart of the B10 is its 4.6-litre eight-cylinder engine. This hand-built powerplant not only produces 253 kW/347 bhp, and the excellent performance that comes with this level of power, but also the kind of refinement expected from a luxury saloon

The V8 propels the BMW ALPINA B10 from a standing start to 100 km/h in just 5.5 seconds (touring 5.7 seconds) and on to a top speed of 279 km/h (touring 269 km/h). Sure, there will be few opportunities to drive at this speed, but the figure shows the abundant

power reserves available if required

The superior unfolding of power is the decisive requirement for utilizing the potential of the B10 V8 safely and in a stress-free manner. The BMW ALPINA

B10 V8 is available as a 5-speed automatic only, yet another contribution to high comfort. However, this does not mean the driver is put into a passive role, for this would definitely not do justice to a BMW ALPINA

The B10 offers two different ways of manually selecting gears. The driver can either put the selector into Steptronic mode or else use ALPINA's own SWITCH-TRONIC system, which features two push buttons mounted behind the steering wheel spokes

Alpina's special 4.6-litre V8 B10 package for the E39 was only available in automatic guise, demonstrating that both Alpina and BMW have moved with the times and changing buyer tastes. Automatics are handier in town! (Courtesy Alpina GB)

The revised E39, in 530i guise, on its debut at the 2001 Paris Auto Salon. Complete with Double Vanos and a nifty 231 chevaux! (Courtesy Paul Baylis)

In 2001 the 5 Series kidney grille actually became wider, although it's hard to tell. (Courtesy Paul Baylis)

rear lamps. More noticeable has been the introduction of Xenon gas discharge lamps, with their spooky ray of blue light!

E39 520D, 525D & 530D – BMW DIESEL DELIGHTS!

Does the E39's ultimate image machine status cover the diesel version? A diesel used to be the sort of car people didn't like to admit to owning in front of family, friends and small children. Consider a mid seventies, US spec Daimler-Benz 240D. Its 2.4-litre four-cylinder put out 62bhp and its 0 to 60 time ran to half a minute. It was very difficult to start

Since the late '70s it has been possible to order almost any 5 Series variant in auto or manual form. This particular car is a 530d. E39 production totalled 1,488,038 5 Series. (Courtesy Paul Baylis)

in cold climates and there was the usual diesel clatter on start-up. *Consumer Union* noted in 1974 that the sound wasn't unlike a spoon caught in a waste disposal unit! It was so loud it alerted the test driver's neighbour, living at the other end of the block, to put on his coat and stand outside for the daily car pool!

Sure, you didn't have to stand in gas station queues at the height of the gas crunch, but that had to be balanced with shorter service intervals and performance that put you in the truck lane. There wasn't anything wrong with the MB 240D, this was just par for the course if you owned a diesel.

The fabulous common rail, direct injection turbo diesel. Initially rated at 184bhp, another German fiscal limit, subsequent revisions saw the figure climb to the next fiscal cut-off point at 193 horses. (Courtesy Paul Baylis)

Nothing stays the same if you are willing to play the R&D game! Today's BMW diesel, as with contemporary diesels, are easier to use, achieve great economy and suffer no performance penalty. Today's bimmer oil burner features direct common rail injection and a variable vane turbo. Diesel is squirted at very high pressure directly into the combustion chamber.

The common rail part of the equation was thought up by Fiat and licked into shape by Bosch. The computer adjusted variable vane turbo alters size in order to achieve optimum effect on the move. Small turbo at low speed to spool up fast and cut lag, big turbo at higher speed to deliver the punch forced induction is known for.

The E39 diesel range involves the four pot 520d and six-cylinder 525d and 530d, with the largest engined version generating 184bhp at 4000rpm and 288 pounds per foot of twist at only 1750rpm. Not enough to match the outright figures of a manual 530i, but plenty to outscore the in-gear acceleration time recorded by the manual 535i V8! With a super tall 2.35 final drive the 530d has a quieter cruising demeanor than petrol E39s. Combine this with 30 to 40mpg overall economy and you have a luxury saloon that's hard to beat. Of course, the diesel versions have to use the V8's recirculating ball steering and the cast iron block six doesn't have ideal weight distribution.

Still, with hefty European petrol prices what the E39 diesels offer could be enough to tip the scales in their favour. It all started in the late seventies when BMW and diesel gurus Steyr-Daimler-Puch worked together on BMW's first diesel. Work on the Austrian factory started in 1979 with production commencing in 1982, the same year that BMW bought out Steyr. It stood BMW in good stead, given the increasing importance diesel power has in continental Europe. When Alpina produces something like the diesel D10 package you know something is up!

The Alpina B10 4.6 V8 was the ultimate automatic E39 5 series. (Courtesy Alpina46)

13

THE RETURN OF A LEGEND, AND A 4X4?

THE E39 M5 COMES ALIVE ... EVENTUALLY

The M5 and cars of its ilk are best not measured by the usual yardsticks. It would be selling them short to do so. It's much better to view them as examples of what can be created when the normal constraints affecting mainstream car design are relaxed.

Why did the E39 M5 take so long to arrive? BMW felt, and not without some reason, that the 540i six-speed with firm suspension was as much as most folks would want. The trouble was that the company's rivals had other ideas. When the final E34 M5 left it was a case of 'while the cat's away the mice will play.' Jaguar's XJR, Daimler-Benz's E class shoe horn specials and Audi's S8 soon took over the town.

Finally, in late 1998, the E39 M5 V8 arrived and it was as if the M5 had never gone on sabbatical. The engineers had created a unique displacement version of the corporate BMW V8. Given

After a three-year hiatus the M5 was back, and bigger than ever with two extra cylinders! It resumed its role at the head of the 5 Series range as if it had never left. (Courtesy Brian Beckmann)

If ever there was a BMW that lived up to the 'Ultimate Driving Machine' slogan, it was the E39 M5. (Courtesy Jason Tang)

The 4.9-litre Motorsport V8 utilised suction pumps to stave off the oil starvation problems experienced by V8s in high speed cornering. (Courtesy Brian Beckmann)

Alpina's B10 V8 4.6, came out prior to BMW's E39 M5. The Buchloe Bandit was slightly slower, but more exclusive. (Courtesy Alpina46)

No E39 M5 Touring, no problem. Just try Hartge for its 350bhp 5-litre H5 Touring V8. It also had thrifty sixes! (Courtesy Hartge)

BMW wasn't the only master of six. AC Schnitzer's later 3.2-powered ACS5s came with 235bhp and 252lb/ft.
(Courtesy AC Schnitzer)

that BMW's V8 has coated bores, one cannot simply do a bore and stroke to bump up displacement. As per tuner Alpina, BMW cast a new block displacing 4.9 litres. The Motorsport V8 had an eleven to one compression ratio and, for the first time on BMW's V8, the Double Vanos variable valve timing. Somehow, the engineers had managed to incorporate hydraulic tappets on the new motor; quite a feat given that high revving engines don't like such compensating devices. It was yet another first for a Motorsport powerplant.

One concern with the V8 layout is oil starvation. In hard cornering the angle of the cylinders can result in the oil accumulating in the valve covers. Suction pumps in the M5's engine draw such accumulated oil. When driving in a straight line the pumps suck oil from the rear of the cylinder head and block, directing it back to the sump. In cornering electromagnetic valves between the pumps, and pick-ups on the outer side of the cylinder head, open to draw wayward oil back to the sump. Such engine saving devices are alerted into action by lateral g forces detected by the M5's traction control.

For an engine designed to live life on the edge, bigger water jackets and extra channels around the intake ports help keep body and soul together. The same role is carried out by a series of yellow warning lights placed on the tach between 4500rpm and the 7000rpm redline. This was a 'keep off the grass' signpost telling the driver to lay off the motor in the early stages of operation. Once warmed up the lights progressively go out and permit fuller use of the V8's 400bhp net. Without the electronic watchdog the engine could be calling for help and you just wouldn't know. In space, they really can't hear you scream!

The observant would notice a dash button marked sport on the dashboard. When activated the M5's fly-by-wire electronic throttle would change over to computer mapping which permitted sharper response to the driver's right hoof. In addition, the power steering pump's valving was altered to cure that numbness which seemed to afflict the helm of V8 powered E39s. The only criticism was that the sharper throttle response and steering came as a pair. Testers noted it would have been nice to have better steering all the time and keep the eager throttle out of the equation whilst in town. Sadly,

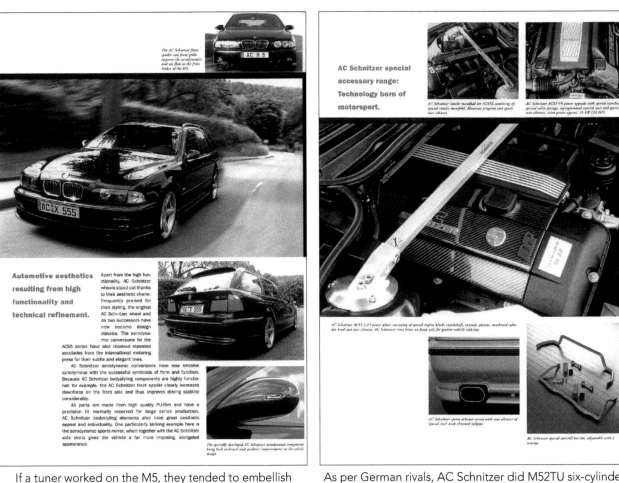

If a tuner worked on the M5, they tended to embellish around Motorsport's hardware. However, with hot Tourings the choice was easy. BMW didn't do hot E39 shooting brakes. (Courtesy AC Schnitzer)

As per German rivals, AC Schnitzer did M52TU six-cylinder and M62 V8 engine packs. However, for E39 diesels Alpina was in charge. (Courtesy AC Schnitzer)

even in such exalted circles there must still be compromise!

The aluminium suspension parts of the E39 were retained but fortified to cope with potentially more onerous duties. The six-speeder, usually found on the 540i, was also roped in for a session of self-improvement. However, testers trying to break the 5-second 0 to 60 barrier quickly found out that you only got a few shots before the clutch said it needed a nap. It was also par for the course to expect the gearbox to have a heavier clutch and notchier shift than that encountered in an E39 528i. Still, a quarter mile time of around 14 seconds, and the standstill sprint to 100mph in under 13 seconds makes the M5 an uncommonly swift luxury saloon.

Safety is never taken lightly at BMW. The M5 drew on the E39's already introduced hardware which included 10 airbags. Side bags accompanied the E39's 1996 introduction and side window units followed in 1997. Massive floating ventilated disc rotors kept the heavyweight M5's speed in check. Even Phil Scott mentioned on Australian television that the car's brakes could easily cope with a fair amount of track work! Even so, one cannot doubt the value of the three-point seatbelt, so belt up! Settle into the leather and alcantara trimmed interior and survey the expensive domain. Whether it is the aluminium of the 'Sportive' or the burr walnut of the 'Exclusive', quality is assured.

The M5's handling has an agresssive edge that motoring journalists welcome, especially after the E36 M3 and Motorsport Z3 which they considered too

MK-Motorsport had supercharger packages for BMW's baby sixes and V8s. By the 2000s, tuners had made their way back to blowers. (Courtesy MK-Motorsport)

For the E39 5 Series, MK-Motorsport did a 5-litre 540i conversion. It rode on these 19in MK-3 rims up to 177mph! (Courtesy MK-Motorsport)

neutral. The M5 still served up oversteer at the limit, but only if you ordered it. In spite of 18-inch rims and 245 section rubber at the front and 275 section footwear at the rear, animal instincts were tempered with civility. It didn't cacoon like a Caddy, but nor did it annoy passengers like a Daimler-Benz E 55. Ride comfort and road roar were kept in check.

The halo effect of a high energy sports saloon was too much for BMW's rivals to ignore. If their creations don't hang together as well as the M5 it could be because the call of the wild took them away from their usual course of business. For BMW the M5 was a natural extension of everyday work of developing excellent sports saloons: think of the E39 M5 as the ultimate 1961 BMW 1500. You are not likely to encounter an inspired engine that isn't on speaking terms with the chassis. From mind-blowing acceleration to the illuminated shifter tip, the M5 has everything covered.

The M5 has a dash mounted 'Sport' button that alters the power steering pump's valving, largely eliminating the dead feeling at the helm associated with E39s that have recirculating ball steering. (Courtesy Mark Odom)

THE E39 TOURING & E53 SUV – INTO NEW TERRITORY

If the M5 related to BMW's established area of expertise, then the E39 Touring marked the Bavarian concern's attempts to reach a wider audience. As with the E34 version, the new 5 Series

The M5 must be one of the most understated cars capable of a 14-second quarter mile time. (Courtesy Brian Beckmann)

The M5's shifter knob is illuminated, and its lighting intensity varies in sync with the rest of the dash lighting. It's the little touches that make all the difference. (Courtesy Gary W Gillespie)

The absence of an autobox, and the ability to turn off the DSC system, emphasises the driver-orientated nature of the M5. (Courtesy Mark Odom)

touring was no load carrier. The designers biased it towards driving pleasure rather than load lugging. Apart from being marginally heavier, and having 45/55 weight distribution, it wasn't far off the superb mark established by the saloons, and there were even some concessions to convenience!

There was the nearly flat load area, a bonus of the E39's less intrusive, multi-link rear suspension. Plus, a lockable underfloor storage area and pull-out load platform that, whilst it wobbled, gave the owner a sporting chance of avoiding a bad back. Even though there wasn't an M5 Touring, as there had been with the E34, this version still had sufficient sports credentials to earn the BMW badge. Alpina certainly thought so; it would hardly have gone to the trouble of offering the six-cylinder B10 3.2 touring if it didn't! As with the diesel, the Buchloe tuner was once again following BMW's moves to meet changing and wider customer demands.

Customers have certainly demanded Sport Utility Vehicles (SUVs) and Multi Purpose Vehicles (MPVs). Indeed, in the nineties the SUV and pick-up truck market flourished in the States, taking over market share from conventional passenger vehicles. BMW wasn't asleep and it wasn't long before its Carolina Spartanburg facility was turning out E53 X5s in addition to the usual 3 Series and Z3s. After all, if the majority of sales are going to come from a particular market it makes good sense to locate close to the action.

The X5 seems to have largely avoided the build problems that plagued early examples of the US-built Daimler-Benz M class. More

Motorsport's three colour livery is one of the few outward indications that this is indeed an M5, and not a regular E39 variant. The sleeper, or Q ship, approach has found favour in recent years with motoring journalists and performance buyers alike. (Courtesy Taylor E Spalt)

The E53 X5 is built in the US, at BMW's Spartanburg, Carolina, plant. It has experienced fewer assembly line defects than its rival, the US built Daimler-Benz M class. (Courtesy Al Burdulis)

The Touring concept returned, as displayed by this 1997 E39 540i Touring V8. The 4.4-litre M62 had a handy torque advantage over the M60 4-litre, but still made 286bhp. (Courtesy Jonathan Beard)

than just a 5 Series on stilts, the model is BMW's interpretation of a recreational vehicle that will spend most of its life on-road. To this end it features unibody construction and no low range gearing, preferring to rely on a hill descent facility to check travel down steep declines. BMW got this feature from Range Rover, during the era when the Bavarians owned Rover. Engine options run from a petrol six, to a much praised direct injection, common rail turbo diesel, and – finally – the 4.4 and 4.6-litre V8 powerhouses. The petrol six was initially, for some markets, the 2.8-litre Double Vanos unit. As at the start of 2001 this was replaced by the 3-litre update of the same motor.

Minimal bodyroll, agility and communicative steering combine to inspire driver confidence. In fact, the X5 is probably the most car-like of its generally highway-loving rivals. However, SUVs are not heavy-duty off roaders and it's best not to get carried away on the loose stuff. Of all the versions the turbodiesel is probably the best compromise. Its abundant torque copes admirably with the X5's not inconsiderable girth, and the diesel part of the equation makes economy tolerable. The V8 variants are quick, but quite thirsty. The six-cylinder petrol unit has impressive outright performance figures, but a lack of torque compromises in-gear work and overtaking.

This X5 4.4 V8 is enjoying a Floridian moment amongst the palm trees. (Courtesy Mark Odom)

Using the same 4.4-litre V8 found in the 5/7/8 series, the X5 4.4 V8 can sprint from 0 to 60 in 7.5 seconds – not bad for one so large. (Courtesy Ozgun Ozguc)

For the X5 4.6iS, BMW's SAV lived up to its badge id, with a 4.6-litre V8 making 340 horses. (Courtesy Greg Smith)

The X5 cabin is a nice place to be. It's light and airy, plus cabin fittings aren't far off the quality of a regular 5 Series. Standard equipment is respectable, and BMW's still substantial options list lets you personalise your new toy. 2001 has seen the arrival of a Sport package for the X5, too, in certain markets. It includes 19-inch hoops, power seats and a stylised wood decorated steering wheel. Take it easy with the options, though. The value for money Sport pack is subsidised by disproportionately pricey options outside the pack.

Well, we have come a long way in our three decade story. The development of the motor car in this period has seen an increasing desire to meet the needs of consumers and a rapidly changing world, and all against a backdrop of increased competition and trouble-free, reduced maintenance motoring. BMW has already put its Valvetronic, no-throttle butterflies future theory into effect with the second generation compact.

There's also talk of a sequential manual gearbox for the next M5, a Motorsport Diesel, and even a baby X3 and giant X7 to join the present X5. It's an exciting future, but one that will always be tempered by compromise. Finite world resources make the choice of personal transport one that requires much consideration. More information will be the first step in making this decision easier.

The E53 X5 4.6iS was an M vehicle in all but name. With the E53, BMW claimed to have invented the SAV, or Sports Activity Vehicle. (Courtesy Greg Smith)

Apart from the missing M badge, the only thing the X5 4.6iS lacked for true 'Motorsportness' was a manual gearbox. Aside from that, Bavarian rappers declared the 4.6iS to be plenty phat ... werd! (Courtesy Greg Smith)

BMW had the foresight to go SUV – pardon me, SAV – early. Others, like Saab and Alfa, missed the trend, to their financial peril. (Courtesy Jack Tulling)

BMW's corporate visage is recognisable to enthusiasts and non-enthusiasts alike, and many of its rivals would like to emulate this brand recognition in such an image conscious market. (Courtesy Paul Baylis)

BMW
DATABASE

MEET THE TUNERS

AC Schnitzer

www.ac-schnitzer.de

AC Schnitzer can trace its ancestry back to racing's Team Schnitzer (1967), founded by brothers Josef and Herbert Schnitzer. The AC moniker arose from the licence plate ID of their Aachen location. The tuner's first formal 5 Series was the 245bhp E28 ACS5. The tuner's popularity took off after 1987, when a distribution deal was struck with BMW super dealer Kohl Automobile GmbH.

Alpina

www.alpina-automobiles.com/de

Alpina was founded by Burkhard Bovensiepen in 1965, the family business-made typewriters bearing the same title. A hop-up kit for the BMW 1500 represented the company's first foray into tuning. Alpina became an official car maker in 1978. With the E39 chassis, Alpina had an exclusively automatic B10 4.6 V8 that predated BMW's E39 M5.

Birds BMW

www.birdsauto.com
Telephone: +44 (0) 1753 657 444
Fax: +44 (0) 1753 655 963

Address: Kevin Bird Garages LTD, 2, The Ridgeway, Iver, Bucks, SL0 9HW, United Kingdom
SatNav- BMW OE use 'Ridge Way, SL0.' Google, use 'Ridgeway SL0 9HW.'

Birds is an independent BMW specialist family run dealership. It has been Hartge's UK agent since the E28 5 Series H5 package of the 1980s. Unlike the contemporary Alpina agent, Sytner, Birds was willing to modify existing cars to customer requirements, rather than just proffer complete turnkey specials. Beyond the Hartge connection, Bird's tuning operation offers a wide range of performance enhancing hardware.

Breyton Design

www.breytonwheels.co.uk

In Stockach 1982, computer tech engineer Edmund Breyton established what became Breyton Design. This high tech background saw the firm use CAD/CAM to create visually exciting alloy wheel designs. Early work even ran to rims and bodykit for independent AMG! These were successfully exported to America and Asia. Eventually a 3.2-litre, six-pot E39 package, with M30 3.4-litre six-cylinder injectors, was realised.

Dinan

www.dinancars.com
Dinan was founded by Steve Dinan in 1979. However, the US tuner first got fame for its turbo M30s and chassis work on US E28s in the 1980s. Dinan carried on its turbo programme with the E34 5 Series in the 1990s, and added supercharger kits to its portfolio, too.

H&B

www.hbspecialists.com
H&B was established in 1974 by Allen Hardy and Hans Beck. Originally a US West Coast Alpina agent, they were selling their own H&B cars by 1980. These E12, E21, E23 & E24 cars were better suited to US spec BMWs, and American driving conditions.

Hamann

www.hamann-motorsport.com
Richard Hamann is an accomplished racing driver on two and four wheels, including the BMW M1. His upmarket tuning house covers the Ferrari and Bentley brands. 5 Series involvement commenced with the E34, and went on to include an E36 M3 Evo engined E39 532i. The firm favours large, normally-aspirated conversions.

Hartge

www.hartge.de/e/home.html
Herbert and Rolf Hartge were brothers with a successful Beckingen BMW dealership. They raced BMWs, bringing their track expertise to Hartge GmbH in 1971. Formally recognised as an automaker from 1983.

Koenig-Specials

www.koenig-specials.com
Koenig-Specials was started by Willy Koenig. Purveyors of modified Ferraris, the tuner commenced with the first Ferrari 365 BB to arrive in West Germany (1974). The company has had 5 Series involvement from the E34 chassis.

MK-Motorsport

www.mk-motorsport.de/html_en/index.html
Was started by racer Michael Krankenberg in July 1978. Earlier, Krankenberg's wild 1976 Group 2 racing car, was reputed to be the most powerful 1602 in Europe! The tuner did E28 bodykit / chassis fettling, and gained 1990s fame for its block pattern alloy wheels.

BMW'S CLASSIC M5S

M535i (1980-81) E12
Engine: 3453cc, 218bhp, M90 I6, Bosch L-Jetronic fuel-injection

Suspension: (front) Independent MacPherson strut, coil, swaybar (rear) Independent semi-trailing arm, telescopic damper, coil, swaybar.

Brakes: (front) 11-inch vent disc (rear) 10.7-inch solid disc

Gearbox: five-speed (close ratio)

Boot capacity: 16cu ft

Length/width/height: 181.9/66.5/56.1 inches

Weight: 2971lb

0-60mph: 7.0 seconds

Top speed:140mph

Overall mpg: 18-24
Report: *Autosport* Feb 1981

M5 (1985-87) E28
Engine: 3453cc, 286bhp, M88/3 I6, Bosch ML-Jetronic fuel-injection

Suspension: (front) Independent MacPherson strut, coil, swaybar, double pivot design (rear) Independent semi-trailing arm, telescopic damper, coil, swaybar. Plus 13 degree rear trail angle & Trac-Link

Brakes: (front) 11.8-inch vent disc (rear) 11.2-inch solid disc + ABS

Gearbox: five-speed overdrive manual

Boot capacity: 16.1cu ft

Length/width/height: 181.9/66.9/55.7 inches

Weight: 3064lb

0-62mph: 6.5 seconds

Top speed: 148mph

Overall mpg: 24.9

Source: BMW factory data

M5 3.8 (1993-95) E34
Engine: 3795cc, 347bhp, S38B38 I6, Bosch DME M3.3 fuel-injection

Suspension: (front) Independent MacPherson strut, coil, swaybar, double pivot design (rear) Independent semi-trailing arm, telescopic damper, coil, swaybar. Plus 13-degree rear trail angle & Trac-Link

Brakes: (front) 13.6-inch vent disc (rear) 12.8in vent disc + ABS

Gearbox: six-speed manual

Pictured in Anza Borrego Springs, south of Los Angeles, is, perhaps, the only gray E34 M5 in the US? (Courtesy Justin Nardone)

(five-speed prior to 1995) – both overdrive

Boot capacity: 16.1cu ft

Length/width/height:

185.8/68.9/55.6 inches

Weight: 3795lb

0-60mph: 5.8 seconds

Top Speed: 166.1mph (in non governed 5th gear)

Overall mpg: 17.7

Source: *CAR* January 1995

M5 (1999-2003) E39
Engine: 4941cc, 400bhp, S62 V8, Siemens MSS 5.2 fuel-injection

Suspension: (front) Independent MacPherson strut, coil, swaybar, double pivot design (rear) Independent multi-link, telescopic damper, coil, swaybar. M5 had reinforced elements compared to normal E39 aluminium suspension

Brakes: (front) 13.6-inch vent disc (rear) 12.9 vent disc + ABS

Gearbox: six-speed manual overdrive

Boot capacity: 16.1cu ft

Length/width/height: 188.3/78.3/56.4 inches

Weight: 3863lb

0-60mph: 5.3 seconds

Top Speed: 161mph (in 6th gear, governed in 5th)

Overall mpg: 13.4

Source: *Autocar* 20th January 1999

BMW STUFF
www.E12.de
The world's number one E12 information and research site. Started by Ulrich Thieme.
www.firstfives.org
US E12 registry and forum,

with international membership. Founded by Gregory Szczyrbak.

www.mye28.com
An enthusiast community for the E28 chassis 5 Series. It includes a technical forum, for repair discussion.

www.E34.de
Devoted to the E34 5 Series, a German site with discussion forums to help E34 owners and fans.

http://thealpinaregister.com
The place to go for Alpina owners, and those seeking info on Alpinas past and present. For the enjoyment of the wares of Herr Bovensiepen!

http://www.hbspecialists.com/
An independent BMW & Mini specialist. H&B started in 1974 by Allen Hardy, was America's first BMW tuner. Today, it offers repair services / parts for new and older BMWs, including its past Alpina/ West and H&B cars.

https://www.wallothnesch.com/
Walloth & Nesch, is a German spare parts order house, specialising in 1961-1982 BMWs (From New Class 1500 to E23 7 Series)

http://www.realoem.com/
BMW online spare parts listing.

GALLERY – BMW'S 1970S RISE TO SUCCESS

1971: Importing agent BMW Concessionaires GB even did RHD conversions on left hooker only BMWs. (Courtesy BMW)

(Above left) 1972: *Mot* magazine previewed BMW's new E12 5 Series. It noted that, unlike German rivals the Opel Commodore and Ford Granada, the E12 lacked a six-cylinder engine. That would change when the 525 came out at the 1973 Frankfurt Auto Show! (Courtesy *Mot*)

(Above) 1974: BMW showing off its steady speed fuel economy. During the first fuel crisis of 1973/74, Britain and West Germany introduced a blanket 50mph speed limit, to save gas. In East Germany, cars had yet to reach 50mph! (Courtesy BMW)

(Left) 1977: The revised Series 2 E12 5 Series, directly took on the new Daimler-Benz W123 saloon. (Courtesy BMW)

1980: BMW itself took on the importation and distribution of BMWs in Britain. More competitive pricing greatly boosted sales in 1980-82. (Courtesy BMW)

1981: The E21 323i joined the E12 M535i and E23 745i Turbo as early '80s North American gray market heroes! (Courtesy BMW)

BMW greeted the '80s...with the BMW E28 5 Series! (Courtesy BMW)

BMW's 1982 E28 528i and E28 518. (Courtesy BMW)

The E28 was the first 5 Series with an angled dash and Service Interval (SI) Indicator System. (Courtesy BMW)

The 90bhp 1982 BMW 518 four-speed entry level model. (Courtesy BMW)

The 347 DIN bhp S38B38 E34 M5 3.8 I6 motor. (Courtesy BMW)

Lagerfeld: Creating a romantic mood with stretch dress and the Marlene Dietrich beret-look.

5-series touring – for leisure.

An enchanted forest, a perfect sky, swaying wheatfields – time for a country outing. Appropriate dress might comprise a light wool coat with narrow shoulders, black piping, patch pockets and gold buttons. The perfect complementary clothing underneath: a tight, calf-length stretch dress with zip. Not forgetting the black beret for that irresistible Marlene Dietrich look. That, in Karl Lagerfeld's eyes, is the outfit that goes with a BMW touring.

For the 1992 spring/summer fashion season, Karl Lagerfeld, Claudia Schiffer and *BMW Magazine* collaborated to dress up BMW drivers. (Courtesy *BMW Magazine*)

Within the image:

3/1992 $6.50

BMW
MAGAZINE

More than meets the eye: the new M5

The all-conquering 1993 model year BMW E34 M5 3.8! (Courtesy *BMW magazine*)

INDEX